CONTENTS

Overview

Chapter One: Refugees

Introduction

Refugees is the eighty-ninth volume in the **Issues** series. The aim of this series is to offer up-to-date information about important issues in our world.

Refugees looks at the issue of refugees and asylum seekers around the world.

The information comes from a wide variety of sources and includes:
Government reports and statistics
Newspaper reports and features
Magazine articles and surveys
Website material
Literature from lobby groups
and charitable organisations.

It is hoped that, as you read about the many aspects of the issues explored in this book, you will critically evaluate the information presented. It is important that you decide whether you are being presented with facts or opinions. Does the writer give a biased or an unbiased report? If an opinion is being expressed, do you agree with the writer?

Refugees offers a useful starting-point for those who need convenient access to information about the many issues involved. However, it is only a starting-point. At the back of the book is a list of organisations which you may want to contact for further information.

*****

Refugees

Information from Refugee Week

Who is a refugee?

2004 is the 53rd anniversary of the 1951 United Nations Convention relating to the status of refugees. 53 years ago, we vowed that the horrors of the Holocaust should never be allowed to occur again. 53 years ago, 134 countries signed an agreement that anyone, anywhere, who found it necessary to flee persecution in their own country could have their claim for asylum heard fairly, and would receive protection if they needed it.

The Convention gave us a clear-cut definition of the word refugee for the first time: a refugee is defined as someone who is forced to leave home and country, who escapes to another country and is given refugee status by the government of that country. For a person to be given refugee status, the government of the country to whom the person has fled must decide whether that person has (of their home country):

'a well-founded fear of being persecuted for reasons of race, religion, nationality, membership of a particular social group or political opinion'.

When a refugee arrives in a new country, they are known as an asylum seeker until they are granted refugee status. If someone has fled their home in fear of their lives but has not crossed the borders of their country, then they are known as an internally displaced person.

Imagine how you would feel if, tomorrow, you had to flee your home and family in fear of your own safety. Who would you turn to? Where would you go? How would you cope?

This is the tragedy that has befallen people all over the world, and yet refugees often rise above their adversity and make a disproportionately rich contribution to the societies they join.

Refugees include many world-famous figures such as . . . Jesus Christ, Dalai Lama, Karl Marx, Lucian Freud, Sigmund Freud, Albert Einstein, Camille Pissarro, Joseph Conrad, Victor Hugo, Carl Djerassi (inventor of the contraceptive pill), Sir Alex Isigonis (designer of the Mini), Lord Hamlyn, Georg Solti, Piet Mondrian, Marc Chagall, Michael Marks (Marks & Spencer), Rabbi Hugo Gryn, Sitting Bull . . . But there are millions of ordinary people. Ordinary people like you and me. Ordinary people in extraordinary circumstances.

Facts and figures

UK

In the year 2002, there were 85,865 new applications for asylum in the UK. The nationalities with the largest numbers of applicants during 2002 were from: Iraq, Zimbabwe, Afghanistan, Somalia and China.

In 2001, by far the majority of asylum applicants came from Afghanistan and Iraq. In 2002, Iraqi nationals made up 17 per cent of all applications lodged. Zimbabwean and Afghan nationals accounted for 9 per cent of all asylum applications in 2002 respectively.

Asylum applications were made from more than 42 countries in 2002.

The most recent figures show that the top five nationalities seeking asylum in the UK are from:

Somalia, China, Iran, Zimbabwe and Iraq

Applications from Somali nationals increased by 60% between June and September 2003, accounting for 12% of the total applications for that period. Applications from Chinese and Iranian nationals both increased by 37% respectively. Other significant increases between June and September 2003 were: Pakistan (31%), Democratic Republic of Congo (27%) and Iraq (9%).

Imagine how you would feel if, tomorrow, you had to flee your home and family in fear of your own safety

---

While the top asylum nationalities clearly reflect the presence of war, a particularly volatile situation or a totalitarian regime, the spectrum of countries from which people flee also indicates the complexity of human rights abuses or other difficult situations from which individuals may have to escape.

World context

The UK hosts a small fraction of the world's refugees. On 1 January 2003, UNHCR (United Nations High Commissioner for Refugees) estimated that there were 20,556,700 'Persons of Concern' throughout the world who fall under their mandate, including 10,389,700 refugees, 1,014,400 asylum seekers and 5,777,200 internally displaced persons.

According to UNHCR, the vast majority of refugees are sheltering in the developing world. Pakistan hosted 1.2 million at the start of 2003, Iran 1.3 million. Asia hosted nearly half of all people of concern

to UNHCR, followed by Africa, which hosted 22%.

Industrialised world

The figures recently published of the 2002 asylum statistics place the UK 8th out of 37 in terms of numbers of asylum seekers received per head of population in industrialised countries: Austria (4.6 claimants per 1000

inhabitants), Norway, Sweden, Switzerland, Ireland, Liechtenstein and Luxembourg all come ahead of us. The UK received 1.9 claimants per 1000 inhabitants.

Asylum decisions

Between January and September 2003, there were 38,540 new asylum applications (an estimated 47,875 individuals) to the UK. Out of these, 37,155 substantive initial decisions were made, and 29% of these were positive.

During 2002-2003, 74% of applications were decided within two months (compared to a target of 65%).

At the end of September 2003, 33,895 asylum seekers received subsistence-only support and 51,810 received accommodation and subsistence support.

■ The above information is from Refugee Week fact pack. For more details visit www.refugeeweek.org.uk

© Refugee Week

Asylum landmarks in Europe

Information from the United Nations High Commissioner for Refugees (UNHCR)

June 1921
The League of Nations, forerunner of the United Nations, establishes the High Commission for Refugees which is mandated principally to help 800,000 Russian refugees.

February 1946
In the wake of World War II, the UN General Assembly establishes the International Refugee Organisation. Between 1947 and 1951 it helps 1,620,000 people, mainly in Germany and Austria.

January 1951
The United Nations High Commissioner for Refugees replaces the IRO and begins work. In July the Convention relating to the Status of Refugees is adopted and provides the most comprehensive codification of

refugee rights in history. The Convention is limited to persons who become refugees before 1 January 1951. States are free to limit refugee claims to victims of events in Europe.

January 1967
A Protocol to the Refugee Convention is adopted, extending protection to all refugees, whatever the date they were forced to leave their countries, and removing the geographical limitation to Europe.

June 1990
Five nations – Belgium, the Netherlands, Luxembourg, France and

Germany – sign the Schengen Implementation Agreement which, when fully implemented five years later, envisages the end of border controls and free travel between member states. All EU member states except Ireland and the UK join by the end of the 1990s.

June 1990
The Dublin Convention (which enters into force in 1997) is the first major step by Europe to coordinate national asylum policies, establishing the responsibility of individual countries to examine asylum requests.

February 1992
The Treaty on European Union (Maastricht) empowers Justice and

Home Affairs Ministers to establish a framework for a Europe-wide asylum policy.

June 1992
Ministers adopt a Resolution on Minimum Guarantees for Asylum Procedures containing a number of safeguards for applicants, but crucially allowing states to set some of these aside in certain circumstances.

November 1994
A model 'readmission agreement' is adopted in Brussels which EU member states can conclude with non-member countries making it possible to send asylum seekers back to countries they had transitted en route to Union territory. Many such bilateral agreements are subsequently signed.

March 1996
A Joint Position on the Harmonised Application of the Definition of the Term 'Refugee' in the Geneva Convention tackles the interpretation of the definition of a refugee. It allows states to follow a restrictive approach favoured by several countries which would bar victims of 'non state' persecution by groups such as armed militias from being granted asylum.

June 1997
The Treaty of Amsterdam (which enters into force in May 1999) provides a detailed legal basis for the harmonisation of common asylum and migration policies.

October 1999
The Tampere Conclusions establish the political objectives of a common asylum policy based on 'the absolute respect for the right to claim asylum' and the 'full and inclusive application' of the 1951 Convention.

1999-2001
The European Commission submits to member states four draft directives and one draft regulation that form the heart of the first phase of asylum harmonisation.

December 2000
The Charter of Fundamental Rights of the European Union enshrines asylum as a basic right within the Union.

July 2001
The first major instrument towards European-wide asylum harmonisation is adopted. The Council Directive establishes burden sharing and minimum protection standards in the event of a mass influx of displaced persons.

June 2002
The Seville Conclusions focus on measures to combat illegal immigration, border management and readmission and return.

January 2003
The second of four Council Directives establishes minimum standards for the reception of asylum seekers including accommodation, health care, education, employment and legal security. States, however, are given the opportunity to opt out of some and reduce or withdraw benefits under certain circumstances.

February 2003
A Council Regulation (Dublin II), essentially a revision of the ineffectual 1990 Dublin Convention, redefines the responsibilities of member states in examining asylum applications.

March 2004
Justice and Home Affairs Ministers agree the text of a Qualification Directive which defines who qualifies as a refugee and who qualifies for a more limited or 'subsidiary' degree of legal protection.

30 April 2004
Two days before 10 new members join the Union, the EU Council agrees the text of the Asylum Procedures Directive covering such issues as rights of appeal and the designation of so-called 'safe' countries. It is the last of the five pieces of legislation designed to harmonise asylum policies among member states.

■ The above information is an extract from *Refugees* Vol. 2 2004, the magazine produced by the United Nations High Commissioner for Refugees (UNHCR).

© United Nations High Commissioner for Refugees (UNHCR)

Global refugee numbers fall

By Sarah Left

The world's refugee population fell last year to its lowest level in a decade, led by returnees to Afghanistan and Angola, the UN's refugee agency announced 17 June 2004.

The total 'population of concern' to UNHCR – including refugees, recently returned refugees, asylum seekers, and those displaced within their home countries – fell to 17.1 million by the end of 2003, down from 20.8 million in 2002.

Refugees in particular – defined as those who have fled across an international border – fell for the second consecutive year. The global refugee population fell by 10%, down from 10.6 million in 2002 to 9.7 million in 2003.

'The statistics are very encouraging, especially for the nearly 5 million people who over the past few years have been able to either go home or to find a new place to rebuild their lives,' said Ruud Lubbers, the United Nations High Commissioner for Refugees. 'For them, these dry statistics reflect a special reality – the end of long years in exile and the start of a new life with renewed hope for the future.'

Mr Lubbers credited international efforts to find long-term solutions to refugee situations that have gone on for years or, in some cases, decades. He said there had been 'unprecedented' levels of voluntary repatriation over the past two years, with some 3.5 million refugees going home, most of them Afghans returning from Pakistan and Iran.

The effects of international efforts to improve the situation in Afghanistan had been felt as far away as Europe, where the numbers of Afghan asylum seekers 'plunged', he said.

'The phenomenal return of Afghans to their homeland over the past few years underscores the benefits of sustained international attention and support for the work of UNHCR and its partners in regions of origin,' Mr Lubbers said.

The number of Afghans seeking asylum in the UK has dropped dramatically over the last few years, from 8,820 in 2001 to just 285 in the first quarter of 2004. In 2002, the government introduced a scheme of special payments to Afghans willing to return home voluntarily. Last year it began enforced removals of families whose asylum applications had failed. In 2002 and 2003, a total of 26,838 Afghans either returned voluntarily or were removed from the UK.

> ### The global refugee population fell by 10%, down from 10.6 million in 2002 to 9.7 million in 2003

Mr Lubbers warned that successful repatriation required continued international support and investment in reconstruction efforts.

The number of asylum seekers worldwide fell 12% to 995,000 in 2003. Afghans remained the largest single nationality seeking asylum, with 2.1 million looking for refuge in 74 countries, followed by Sudanese and Burundians.

Pakistan came top of the list of countries for asylum, with 1.1 million seeking refuge there. Next on the list are Iran, Germany, Tanzania and the US, which has 452,500 asylum seekers.

Six countries – Sudan, Liberia, Central African Republic, Congo, Ivory Coast and Somalia – still provided particular cause for concern in 2003: UNHCR currently has 100,000 Sudanese refugees in its camps in eastern Chad, with up to 90,000 more awaiting removal from the insecure Chad-Sudan border region. The agency said hundreds more refugees are arriving every week in Chad, fleeing Arab militia attacks in western Sudan's Darfur region.

On 16 June 2004, UN investigators announced that more than 22,000 refugees had fled fighting in eastern Congo and escaped to neighbouring Burundi in the past week alone. The latest exodus was sparked by a rebel takeover of the eastern town of Bukavu. The government has retaken the town, but tensions remain high in a country still shattered by the 1998-2002 civil war.

Asylum seeker numbers

Estimated number of asylum seekers, refugees and others of concern to UNHCR – 1 Jan 2004

Asia	6,187,800
Africa	4,285,100
Europe	4,268,000
Latin America & Caribbean	1,316,400
Northern America	962,000
Oceania	74,100
Total	**17,093,400**

Source: UNHCR

Refugees and displaced persons

Who

A refugee is someone with a well-founded fear of persecution on the basis of his or her race, religion, nationality, membership in a particular social group or political opinion, who is outside of his or her country of nationality and unable or unwilling to return. Refugees are forced from their countries by war, civil conflict, political strife or gross human rights abuses. There were an estimated 14.9 million refugees in the world in 2001 – people who had crossed an international border to seek safety – and at least 22 million internally displaced persons (IDPs) who had been uprooted within their own countries.

What

Enshrined in Article 14 of the 1948 Universal Declaration of Human Rights is the right 'to seek and to enjoy in other countries asylum from persecution'. This principle recognises that victims of human rights abuse must be able to leave their country freely and to seek refuge elsewhere. Governments frequently see refugees as a threat or a burden, refusing to respect this core principle of human rights and refugee protection.

Where

The global refugee crisis affects every continent and almost every country. In 2001, 78 per cent of all refugees came from 10 areas: Afghanistan, Angola, Burma, Burundi, Congo-Kinshasa, Eritrea, Iraq, the Palestinian territories, Somalia and Sudan. Palestinians are the world's oldest and largest refugee population, and make up more than one-fourth of all refugees. Asia hosts 45 per cent of all refugees, followed by Africa (30 per cent), Europe (19 per cent) and North America (5 per cent).

When

Throughout history, people have fled their homes to escape persecution.

In the aftermath of World War II, the international community included the right to asylum in the 1948 Universal Declaration of Human Rights. In 1950, the Office of the United Nations High Commissioner for Refugees (UNHCR) was created to protect and assist refugees, and, in 1951, the United Nations adopted the Convention Relating to the Status of Refugees, a legally binding treaty that, by February 2002, had been ratified by 140 countries.

Why

In the past 50 years, states have largely regressed in their commitment to protect refugees, with the wealthy industrialised states of Europe, North America and Australia – which first established the international refugee protection system – adopting particularly hostile and restrictive policies. Governments have subjected refugees to arbitrary arrest, detention, denial of social and economic rights and closed borders. In the worst cases, the most fundamental principle of refugee protection, nonrefoulement, is violated, and refugees are forcibly returned to countries where they face persecution. Since September 11, many countries have pushed through emergency anti-terrorism legislation that curtails the rights of refugees.

How

Human Rights Watch believes the right to asylum is a matter of life and death and cannot be compromised. In our work to stop human rights abuses in countries around the world, we seek to address the root causes that force people to flee. We also advocate for greater protection for refugees and IDPs and for an end to the abuses they suffer when they reach supposed safety. Human Rights Watch calls on the United Nations and on governments everywhere to uphold their obligations to protect refugees and to respect their rights – regardless of where they are from or where they seek refuge.

■ The above information is from Human Rights Watch's website which can be found at www.hrw.org
© *Human Rights Watch*

Questions about refugees and asylum seekers

Information from the Refugee Council

Where do asylum seekers come from?

The top 4 countries that asylum seekers arriving in the UK have fled from are:

- Afghanistan
- Iraq
- Somalia
- Sri Lanka

Together, these 4 countries account for a massive 39% of UK asylum applications.*

These are countries ravaged by war or with appalling human rights records. They are all places where persecution occurs, and has been well documented.

The vast majority of asylum seekers flee from the world's trouble spots. The numbers of asylum seekers

arriving in the UK inevitably reflects the international situation at any one time.

What problems do they face?

Asylum seekers often arrive traumatised by their experiences of persecution, torture and flight. In addition, when they reach the UK, they have a set of new problems to contend with . . .

- Language barriers
- Isolation
- Lack of good quality legal advice
- Detention centres
- Racism
- Living 30% below the poverty line

Asylum seekers are NOT allowed to work whilst in the UK. Yet they are expected to live on 70% of income support.

In December 2001, a total of 1,410 asylum seekers were being detained. These are the highest detention figures in Europe. The largest nationality among asylum detainees was Zimbabwean.**

Alphonse was accosted on the way to the supermarket in Leeds by three men.

The men subjected him to a barrage of verbal abuse for being a refugee. Alphonse lied and said he was a student, hoping they would leave him alone, but the abuse continued, so he tried to run away.

Only a short distance from the supermarket, a car stopped in front of him and the three men got out. This time, they held a knife to his throat and demanded to know whether he was a refugee. Terrified, Alphonse denied this several times as the knife was held with increasing pressure against his throat. Finally, he managed to break away and immediately went to the Police.

Unfortunately, racist attacks on asylum seekers are increasing. 297 instances of racial harassment were reported within a recent 3-month period, and many more go unreported.***

References

*   Figures from Home Office Asylum Statistics 2001
**   Figures from Home Office Research Development & Statistics Directorate
***   Figures from Parliamentary Questions, November 2001.

- The above information is from the Refugee Council. For further information, see their address details on page 41.

Sherzad Ali is a refugee from Afghanistan

His 'crime' was to join an underground sect, which set up classrooms and libraries in secret basements to educate women. The Taliban retaliated by publicly executing, shooting dead in the street or simply 'vanishing' those involved. When Sherzad was warned he would be next, he escaped into Pakistan dressed as a woman. In reprisal, the Taliban killed his mother and 24-year-old brother, and sent spies after him. He paid a trafficker to get him to Europe, and now lives in a Birmingham tower block.

'All people have different opinions about foreigners and they should be allowed to have them', he says. 'But believe me – I am only here because I would be killed if I went back home. For the first time in years I feel safe, and for that I will be eternally grateful to the British. You are to me, the finest, most civilised people in the world.'

Fleeing the fighting

Three out of four applications for asylum made by people from countries in conflict, says new report released to mark Refugee Week 2004

Fleeing the Fighting: How conflict drives the search for asylum, is a report released on 14 June 2004 to mark the start of Refugee Week (14-20 June 2004). It reveals how conflict causes people to flee their homes, friends and family to seek sanctuary in other countries, including the UK.

The report also reveals the impact these conflicts have on asylum claims to the UK. According to available Home Office statistics, up to three-quarters (around 74%) of asylum applications are made by people from countries where conflicts are occurring, as defined by the International Institute of Strategic Studies.[1]

Conflict is just one of the global causes of forced migration and displacement, and many people around the world still face persecution in countries that are not at war, such as Zimbabwe, where human rights abuses are well documented. People also flee conflict countries for other human rights reasons.

The report, from organisations including Amnesty International, Refugee Action, Refugee Council and Save the Children,[2] examines conflicts around the world and their impact on civilians.

Disturbing reports from seven countries currently caught up in conflict, and refugees' own personal stories of how they came to seek sanctuary in Britain, provide a stark reminder of who asylum seekers are and why they are here.

Conflict in Sudan, for example, has forced around four million people from their homes. Over half a million have fled Sudan, mainly to neighbouring countries. Tens of thousands live in squalid camps in Chad. Only a fraction of this total, around 930 Sudanese people, applied for asylum in the UK last year.

Speaking on behalf of the agencies, Refugee Council Chief Executive Maeve Sherlock said:

Amnesty International

'People are not choosing to leave – they are choosing to live. Faced with the prospect of death, or rape and torture at the hands of soldiers and armed militia, millions of people every year flee their homes.

'As tough policies and hostile attitudes make it ever more difficult to seek asylum in Britain, this report is a timely reminder of one of the main reasons people come here seeking protection – conflict. Refugees are people forced to flee their homes in fear of their lives – this is a fact that is all too often overlooked.

'The international safety-net of refugee protection is needed more than ever. Refugee Week celebrates both the UK's tradition of offering sanctuary to people fleeing conflict, persecution and other human rights abuses, and the positive contribution that refugees have made and continue to make to the UK.'

The report focuses on war and conflict to reflect the theme of Refugee Week 2004.[3] It examines conflicts in seven key refugee-producing countries around the world – Afghanistan, Colombia, Democratic Republic of Congo, Iraq, Russia, Somalia and Sudan – and the impact of the conflicts on civilians and on the movement of refugees:

Afghanistan

Widespread factional fighting and insecurity continues after 23 years of conflict. Rape and violence by armed factions.

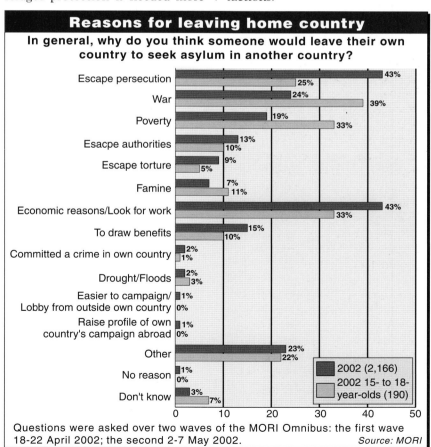

Reasons for leaving home country

In general, why do you think someone would leave their own country to seek asylum in another country?

Reason	2002 (2,166)	2002 15- to 18-year-olds (190)
Escape persecution	43%	25%
War	24%	39%
Poverty	19%	33%
Escacpe authorities	13%	10%
Escape torture	9%	5%
Famine	7%	11%
Economic reasons/Look for work	43%	33%
To draw benefits	15%	10%
Committed a crime in own country	2%	1%
Drought/Floods	2%	3%
Easier to campaign/ Lobby from outside own country	1%	0%
Raise profile of own country's campaign abroad	1%	0%
Other	23%	22%
No reason	1%	0%
Don't know	3%	7%

Questions were asked over two waves of the MORI Omnibus: the first wave 18-22 April 2002; the second 2-7 May 2002.   *Source: MORI*

Colombia

More than 3,000 civilians were killed for political motives in 2003. The military, paramilitaries and guerrilla groups have all been implicated. At least 600 'disappeared' and around 2,200 people were kidnapped as part of the long-running internal armed conflict.

Democratic Republic of Congo

More than three million killed and another 3.4 million uprooted from their homes since 1998 in fighting between government forces and rebel groups.

Iraq

Hundreds of civilians killed by armed groups and coalition forces since the end of the US-led war. Women and girls increasingly face violent attacks including rape, murder and abduction.

Russia

Killings and other human rights abuses by all sides of the conflict in Chechnya have caused tens of thousands of Chechens to flee to neighbouring Ingushetia and other countries.

Somalia

No rule of law or security after 12 years of conflict and state collapse. Hundreds of thousands displaced. Fighting between factions in the capital continues to claim civilian lives.

Sudan

Millions killed and millions more displaced. Renewed fighting in Darfur region has displaced around a million people, many fleeing Sudan altogether.

Notes

1 Figure based on Home Office statistics for 2003, and 'Conflict countries' on current armed conflicts identified by the International Institute of Strategic Studies (IISS).
The IISS definition of armed conflict includes:
- international armed border and territorial conflict involving governments in armed conflict over sovereignty territory;
- internal armed conflicts taking place between government forces and organised groups, which control sufficient territory to sustain concerted military operations; and
- 'terrorist' attacks involving one or more factions in significant armed opposition to a state. The intensity of violence in such attacks varies. Violence directly attributable to organised crime is not included.

2 Refugee Week is a partnership project involving the UK's leading charities that work with refugees. These include:
- Amnesty International UK,
- British Red Cross,
- International Rescue Committee UK,
- Refugee Action,
- Refugee Council,
- Save the Children,
- Scottish Refugee Council,
- Student Action for Refugees (STAR),
- UNHCR, and
- Welsh Refugee Council.
For more information visit www.refugeeweek.org.uk

3 Refugee Week features a programme of events around the country from concerts, exhibitions, football tournaments and film screenings to talks and seminars, helping to demonstrate the positive contribution made by refugees to the United Kingdom.

■ The above information is from Amnesty International's website which can be found at www.amnesty.org.uk

© *Amnesty International*

Internal displacement

Internal Displacement: A Global Overview of Trends and Developments in 2003

With nearly 25 million people uprooted within their own country by conflicts and human rights violations1, internal displacement is one of the great human tragedies of our time. Yet the global crisis of internal displacement, which affects 52 countries across all continents, has unfolded largely unnoticed by the general public. International public attention continues to focus on refugees, i.e. people who crossed international borders after fleeing their homes. In comparison, internally displaced people (IDPs) have received much less attention, although their number

Global IDP
PROJECT

is nearly twice as high, and their plight is often even worse than that of refugees.

Among the millions of people newly displaced in 2003, many were deliberately targeted by their own governments. In several cases, the protection of displaced people was undermined in the context of counter-insurgency campaigns intensified under the guise of the 'war on terror'. Others became victims of attacks by rebel groups or were forced to flee communal violence.

Little tangible progress was made in 2003 with regard to the provision of protection and assistance to internally displaced people. With few exceptions, national authorities continued to be unable or unwilling to fully meet their obligation under international law to protect and assist people displaced within their countries. Neither has the international humanitarian community made the necessary resources available to address the needs of IDPs; nearly a third of IDPs are fully or partially ignored by the UN. The UN system has yet to create the capacity needed for the effective coordination of its response to internal displacement.

Millions of newly displaced people

In 2003, more than three million people were newly displaced, the majority by civil wars and inter-communal violence in Africa. Some 700,000 people were uprooted in the east of the Democratic Republic of Congo (DRC) alone, following a flare-up of violence in the power vacuum left by the withdrawal of foreign occupation troops from neighbouring countries. Intensified fighting in Uganda's civil war forced an equally high number of people to flee their homes. And as Sudan was heading towards a peace agreement between the government and the rebel-controlled south, a new conflict broke out in the western Darfur region, displacing more than half a million people. Other countries with major new displacements include Liberia, Colombia, the Central African Republic, the Philippines and Indonesia.

At the end of 2003, Sudan was the country hosting the largest internally displaced population, some 4 million people. The Democratic Republic of Congo (3 million), Colombia (2.9 million), Uganda (1.2 million), Iraq (1.1 million) and Burma (up to one million) are also among the countries with the highest numbers of internally displaced people.

Peace processes raise hope for return

On the positive side, some three million people were able to return to their homes during 2003, most of them in Angola (1.9 million) and Indonesia (500,000). Thus, the large number of new displacements in 2003 coincided with a similarly high number of returns. These figures do not reflect, however, that many returnees faced enormous difficulties when resettling or returning to their place of origin, including continued serious violations of their human rights, as well as economic destitution.

In 2003, more than three million people were newly displaced, the majority by civil wars and inter-communal violence in Africa

---

A growing number of peace processes raised hope for an improvement of the IDP situation in a number of countries during 2003, including in Liberia, Sudan, Burundi, the DRC, the Balkans, Angola, Sierra Leone, Sri Lanka, Indonesia and several other countries. In some countries, however, progress in the settlement of conflicts was overshadowed by the outbreak or intensification of other crises which led to new displacement. This was, for example, the case in

Darfur in western Sudan, in the Ituri province in eastern DRC, and in Indonesia's Aceh province. In a total of twelve countries, return movements and new displacements took place in parallel.

It was widely feared that the conflict in Iraq, which dominated the internal agenda in 2003, would cause the displacement of several hundred thousand people. This fear, as it turned out, was exaggerated. With some 80,000 people forced to flee, the number of displacements in connection with the military intervention by the United States did not reach such dramatic proportions. In addition, many of those previously displaced under Saddam Hussein's regime were able to return to their homes. Continued insecurity and limited humanitarian access, however, made it difficult to create conditions for durable reintegration.

Apart from the war in Iraq, no new major armed conflict erupted in 2003. But while international attention remained focus on Iraq, numerous other conflicts continued around the world – many with far worse humanitarian consequences.

■ The above information is an extract from *Internal Displacement: A Global Overview of Trends and Developments in 2003* by the Global IDP Project and is also available in pdf format. For further information visit their website which can be found at www.idpproject.org

© The Global IDP Project

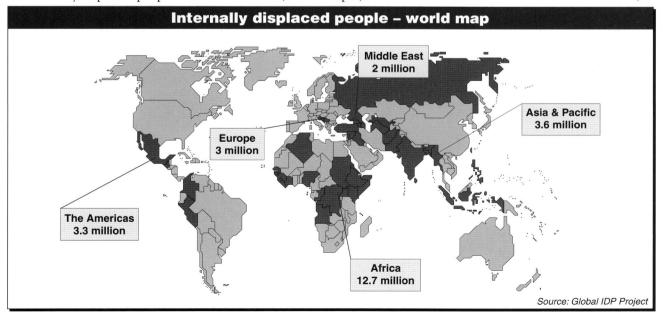

Internally displaced people – world map

Middle East
2 million

Asia & Pacific
3.6 million

Europe
3 million

The Americas
3.3 million

Africa
12.7 million

Source: Global IDP Project

Asylum

Ten questions and answers

What is the scale of the problem?

From 1992 to 1997 about 30,000 applications were received each year. This number rose sharply to 84,000 in 2002 before falling to about 50,000 in 2003.

These totals do not include dependants. The Home Office only counts dependants who arrive before the initial decision on asylum is taken. These dependants added 30% to the totals. Other dependants, fiancés and spouses follow later but are not identified as such in Home Office statistics.

Why do so many come to Britain?

The Home Affairs Committee of the House of Commons in their report 'Border Controls' (January 2001), identified the following 'pull factors':

- family, cultural and historical links
- English language
- job prospects
- availability and perception of social security benefits
- more generous interpretation of asylum law
- slow decision-making on asylum cases
- lack of an efficient removal system for people refused asylum
- access to public services such as free health, education and housing
- scope for living in the country without documentation
- general economic prosperity

Is Britain a 'soft touch' compared to Europe?

Obviously. That is why asylum seekers are queuing up at Channel Ports. In 2002, with 104,000 applicants, including dependants, we were top, ahead of the USA with 81,000. Germany had 71,000, France 51,000 and Italy and Spain had 7,000 and 6,000 respectively. (All figures include dependants.) The number of applications is expected to reduce

by 40% in 2003 but we are still likely to receive more than any other industrialised country.

There are 4 major reasons for this:

- The prospects of being granted asylum are higher. In Germany 9% of applicants are granted asylum or humanitarian protection; in Britain, nearly 37% are granted asylum or its close equivalent Exceptional Leave to Remain (ELR).
- Even if the application fails, there is no effective removal system.

Nearly nine out of ten stay in Britain. And those with families continue to receive benefits worth an average of £16,000 a year tax free.

- The process of decision making takes so long that applicants can, and do, disappear into their own communities, often in city centres. Thereafter, they can live without documentation and can benefit from free health, education and housing. In Germany and France, for example, police carry out sweeps, examining documents and deporting illegal immigrants.
- There are no effective checks on illegal employment. In 2001 only one employer was successfully prosecuted. Asylum seekers can therefore work to repay the cost

Where do asylum seekers come from?

There is quite a wide geographical spread. In the year 2002 the breakdown was:

Europe		13,200
of which		
former Yugoslavia	2,700	
Romania	1,200	
Turkey	2,800	
former USSR	2,700	
Poland	1,000	
Africa		29,400
of which		
Somalia	6,500	
Zimbabwe	7,700	
Dem. Republic of Congo	2,200	
Middle East		18,300
of which		
Iraq	14,600	
Iran	2,600	
Rest of Asia		20,800
of which		
Afghanistan	7,200	
Sri Lanka	3,100	
China	3,700	
Pakistan	2,400	
India	1,900	
Others		2,400
Total		**84,100**

of their passage, sometimes extortionate, or to send money home.

Are asylum seekers 'genuine'?

From 1997-2002 only about 21% of the cases decided were granted asylum (including on appeal). Another 16% were allowed to stay, mainly because of difficulties in returning them – for example to Somalia.

81% are males with an average age of 27.

What happens to those refused asylum?

Most stay on anyway.

At 2003 rates about 60,000 should be removed but only 17,000 will be (including dependants in both cases). This is consistent with past patterns. In the 10 years 1991 to 2000, 240,000 applicants were refused but only 44,000 were removed or departed voluntarily. The Home Office claim that others leave without telling them but there is no evidence of this occurring on a significant scale.

This, naturally, is a major incentive for others to come to Britain.

What does the asylum system cost?

The Home Office estimate for the year 2002 was £1,800 million plus £176 million for legal aid.

What about illegal immigrants?

Illegal immigrants are those who enter the country clandestinely or on forged documents.

It is, by definition, impossible to be sure of the numbers but 50,000 were detected in 2002. An estimate of 50,000 a year for undetected illegal immigrants would, therefore, be conservative.

There is a connection with asylum since many of those who are detected claim asylum; they know that the process is long drawn out and that they can, if necessary, subsequently disappear.

There is a further connection since, if the asylum procedures were to be successfully tightened up, many

would remain illegal rather than apply for asylum. The Government's decision to deny state benefits to those who do not apply 'as soon as reasonably practical' may have this effect.

What is the outlook?

Some of the key 'pull factors' mentioned in question 2 cannot be changed – for example, the English language – or should not, such as general economic prosperity.

Others are likely to strengthen – such as the existence of family links.

The pool of those who might wish to come to Britain is enormous. The top 10 countries of origin have a combined population of 2.73 billion.

The trend has been sharply upward for 5 years. Radical measures will be needed if it is to be reversed.

What can be done?

Within the present legal framework, we can only seek to reduce the 'pull factors' identified in the answer to the second question.

This would involve:
- Clearer identification and recording of claimants.
- Speeding the process to reduce the scope for 'disappearing'.
- Acting against employers of illegal labour.
- A massive increase in the number of removals.

- Action to reduce widespread fraud in connection with National Insurance numbers.
- Measures to ensure that only those entitled have access to health and other services.
- Effective arrangements with our European partners to return applicants to the first country of refuge.
- The introduction of Entitlement Cards.
- Imposing a penalty on the 70% of applicants who are believed to destroy their documents to impede their removal.
- Increasing development aid to improve conditions in source countries.
- Increasing our contribution to the UNHCR which runs refugee camps.

The Asylum and Immigration Act 2002 seeks to accelerate the legal processes, as does the Asylum and Immigration Bill introduced in December 2003, but, without a major increase in removals, this is futile. The 2002 Act also provides for Accommodation Centres but the three proposed will fill in ten days. Nor will there be anything to prevent applicants from disappearing if they anticipate refusal.

- The above information is from MigrationWatch UK's website: www.migrationwatchuk.org

© MigrationWatch UK

Refugees in the UK

Information from Student Action for Refugees (STAR)

What happens to refugees when they arrive in the UK?

Refugees must be granted refugee status by the UK Government before they are allowed to settle and start a new life in this country. Before this occurs they are known as an asylum seeker and are required to follow certain rules and regulations. The current asylum system is complex and the process of getting refugee status lengthy and often confusing.

Levels of support

Asylum seekers are not allowed to find paid employment until they have received a positive decision about their asylum claim. This means that most asylum seekers are dependent on the Government for support while they wait for a decision from the Home Office, even if they are qualified and/or are willing and able to work.

The support an asylum seeker receives depends partly on their personal circumstances (age, marital status, special needs) but also on how quickly they applied for asylum after arriving in the UK.

On 8th January 2003, the Government implemented Section 55 of the Nationality, Immigration and Asylum Act 2002. This means that asylum seekers arriving in the UK are not able to apply for support from the Government (basic living costs and accommodation) unless they apply for asylum as quickly as possible (at port of entry). Anyone applying once in-country (i.e. not on arrival to an immigration officer at port of entry) must provide evidence as to why they did not apply sooner.

The means that new arrivals are often denied automatic access to essential food, shelter and clothing and are being forced into destitution and homelessness.

The rule does not apply to families with children under the age of 18. However, people left without food and shelter do include pregnant

women (until their babies are born) and teenage children who arrive without parents and who the Home Office believe to be over 18.

Those people who claim asylum immediately will be entitled to:

- Accommodation on a no-choice basis either in an accommodation centre or in a 'dispersal' area (designated cities around the country to ease pressure on the South East).
- Cash support received weekly from post offices, at levels 30% less than those received by UK residents on income support.

Detention

Some asylum seekers are detained in specified centres or in prisons upon arrival in the UK. Detainees are denied freedom of movement or access to quality legal advice and are often kept for long periods of time without explanation. Britain's routine use of detention has been condemned by UNHCR, Amnesty International and the British Medical Association.

The decision to detain an individual is made by an Immigration Officer at the air/sea port and is often completely arbitrary. No other European country uses such wide-ranging powers to lock up asylum seekers. Despite the fact that detention costs approximately £15 million per year, the Government are creating new detention centres for asylum seekers.

Waiting for a decision

The process of assessing an individual asylum claim can take up to 2 years, a period during which asylum seekers must simply await a decision made by the Home Office (sometimes in detention or whilst destitute).

Once a decision has been made, an asylum seeker is either:

- granted refugee status or other leave to remain and expected to find their own means of support or apply for income support entitlement within 14 days of receiving their decision
- or subject to detention and deportation from the country regardless of how long they have been in the UK or what life they have made for themselves.

- The above information is from the Student Action for Refugees (STAR) website: www.star-network.org.uk

© Student Action for Refugees (STAR)

The asylum process

Information from the Immigration Advisory Service

How and where can an asylum application be made?

It is not possible to enter the UK in a legal way in order to claim asylum. Asylum can only be claimed from inside the UK. Once inside the UK, an asylum application can be made at a police station, at the Home Office in Croydon or a claim can be made to an immigration officer. It is crucial for an asylum-seeker to claim asylum as soon as possible, preferably upon entry into the UK. If an asylum application is not made as soon as an asylum-seeker enters the UK, they may be denied welfare support and accommodation and it may be detrimental to their claim later on. An asylum application can be made without using the words 'asylum' or 'persecution'. All that is necessary is that the immigration officer, or whomever the claim is made to, understands that the claimant is afraid of return to the country from which they have fled.

What happens after the initial claim for asylum?

There are currently several different ways in which asylum applications are processed. All these ways involve an interview with staff from the Home Office. Often there will be an initial 'screening interview' in which the Home Office only takes the personal details of the applicant and gives that person a reference number for their application. The 'substantive interview', or 'asylum interview', when the applicant gets an opportunity to describe what happened to them and what it is he or she fears, is held some time afterwards. Some applicants are taken to the Oakington Reception Centre, where their application is 'fast-tracked'. They are held in detention while a decision is made on their application within seven days. Some applicants are detained at Harmondsworth detention centre in London, where claimants will be detained throughout their

application and appeal. The entire process usually takes only four to six weeks.

What happens if an asylum-seeker fails to do as the Home Office asks?

Some asylum-seekers risk receiving a 'non-compliance refusal' if they fail to act as the Home Office requires, for example by failing to meet the deadline for the return of a Statement of Evidence Form (SEF). An SEF is usually given to asylum-seekers following the making of the initial claim. If an asylum-seeker fails to meet the conditions imposed by the Home Office for Temporary Admission, for example by failing to attend a scheduled interview, then the asylum-seeker could be refused asylum or could even be taken into detention. If an asylum-seeker has been refused asylum (see below) and fails to meet the ten-day time limit for lodging an appeal, the asylum-seeker can be removed from the country.

It is strongly advisable for an asylum-seeker to do everything the Home Office asks. If possible, an asylum-seeker should seek legal advice before trying to take any complicated steps themselves, such as completing an SEF or lodging an appeal. If legal advice cannot be found in the short time available, the asylum-seeker should try to fill

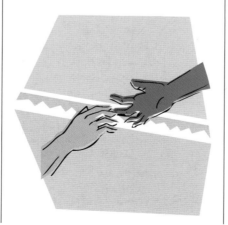

in the forms themselves and then write on the forms that they have not had any assistance in filling them in.

How long does it take to get a decision after an application has been made?

The length of time taken to reach decisions is being reduced at the moment. In previous years an asylum-seeker would often have to wait for two years or more. The Home Office intends for a decision to be made in two months and this target is often achieved for new applications. For those detained at Oakington, the time taken is less than one week. At Harmondsworth, it takes even less time.

What happens to an asylum-seeker whose application has been refused?

Some asylum-seekers have a right of appeal to the courts. Some do not automatically have a right to an appeal inside the UK, if they come from certain countries listed by the Home Office. At the time of writing those countries are the European Union 'accession states' (Republic of Cyprus, Czech Republic, Estonia, Hungary, Latvia, Lithuania, Malta, Poland, the Slovak Republic and Slovenia) and several other countries recently added to the list (Albania, Serbia and Montenegro [including Kosovo], Jamaica, Moldova and Romania). Claims by citizens of these countries are presumed to be clearly unfounded and they are only entitled to appeal from outside the UK. In exceptional cases, claimants from the above countries may be permitted an appeal from inside the UK.

At an appeal, an independent adjudicator who is not employed by the Home Office hears the appeal. The Home Office intends all appeals to be heard within two months of the initial decision. For those asylum-seekers who have had their decision 'fast-tracked' and have been sent to

Oakington or Harmondsworth, the appeal is heard around four weeks after the initial decision.

Once this appeal has been heard, the decision usually arrives within two weeks. After that, some asylum-seekers will be able to appeal further and others will not. It is only possible to appeal further, to the Immigration Appeals Tribunal (IAT), on a point of law, and legal advice will be necessary to decide whether it is possible to appeal. Some asylum-seekers have their claims 'certified' by the Home Office, which means they may not be able to appeal to the IAT. The only means of challenge in such circumstances is the legal process called judicial review. Often adjudicators overturn these certificates, which allows the asylum-seeker to appeal further.

Is asylum easy to get in the UK?

The statistics suggest that asylum is not easy to get in the UK. Estimates differ but it is thought that between 50% and 75% of all applicants are refused and lose their appeal. Each individual asylum-seeker has his or her case assessed on its own facts. There is no quota for the acceptance or refusal of applications or appeals. If an asylum-seeker has a reasonably likely account that suggests s/he would be in genuine danger should s/he be returned to their country, that asylum-seeker has a good chance of getting asylum in one form or another.

How does an asylum-seeker live in the UK while the asylum application is being considered or while he or she is appealing against a refusal?

Most asylum applicants are given what is called 'Temporary Admission', which means they are allowed to live freely in the UK on the condition that they live at a certain address and that they report to a certain police station or immigration officer either weekly or monthly. Asylum-seekers should always inform the Home Office if they move address.

Some asylum applicants are detained. This only happens to a relatively small number of applicants. If the Home Office does decide to

detain an applicant, it will usually be because they believe that the person will fail to maintain voluntary contact with the Home Office and will disappear. The Home Office tends to believe this of asylum-seekers who use deception, for example by using false identity documents once inside the UK (using false documents to enter the UK should not be penalised in this way) or by failing to declare themselves as asylum-seekers as soon as they have entered the country.

If the Home Office believes that an asylum seeker has not made a claim for asylum as soon as reasonably possible after arrival in the UK, the Home Office can refuse to grant support or accommodation to the applicant. However, support and accommodation must be provided if the applicant will have to live in inhuman or degrading circumstances otherwise. Being homeless does not automatically amount to inhuman or degrading treatment, although one or more days of homelessness may well quickly become so. At the time of writing this Government policy is under legal challenge.

For those asylum-seekers who do receive welfare support from the Government, the scheme is administered by the National Asylum Support Service (NASS). Asylum-seekers can also be allocated accommodation by NASS, almost always somewhere in the north of England or in Scotland. It is almost impossible to secure accommodation in London or the south east through NASS. Parents and dependent children (under 18) are allocated accommodation together and NASS

can usually allocate relatives accommodation in the same town or region. If NASS refuses to offer support to an asylum-seeker or refuses to continue giving support, an asylum-seeker does have a right of appeal against that decision. It is best to contact a Citizens' Advice Bureau or local Refugee Council centre for the details of how to do this.

Are there any ways in which an asylum-seeker can increase their chance of success?

Perhaps the best way an asylum-seeker can increase his or her chances of success is by claiming asylum as soon as he or she enters the country, at the place they enter the country, and by seeking legal advice as soon as possible. There are several organisations and firms of solicitors that can offer free assistance to asylum-seekers, including IAS, providing the asylum-seeker meets certain criteria as set out by the Legal Services Commission.

It is very helpful to an application if an asylum-seeker can provide some sort of evidence of the things he or she has suffered or anything that suggests their account is true. Such documents are helpful, but they are not essential for a successful asylum application. It is very important that all asylum-seekers tell the truth when they are claiming asylum, as the Home Office and adjudicators are very good at noticing inconsistencies and have access to a lot of information about the countries from which asylum-seekers come. The Home Office also employs experts in distinguishing real from forged documents.

■ The above information is no substitute for proper legal advice given by a qualified practitioner and is intended only as a basic outline of the law on asylum and on the asylum process, not as a guide to seeking asylum in the UK.

■ The above information is from the Immigration Advisory Service's website which can be found at www.iasuk.org Alternatively, see page 41 for their address details.
© Immigration Advisory Service

Introduction to asylum in Europe

Information from the European Council on Refugees and Exiles (ECRE)

How many people apply for asylum in Europe?

In 2002 381,623 people applied for asylum in the European Union – a decrease of 1.7% (6,749) in applications on 2001 when there were 388,372 applications in the EU. Since 1999 there has been an overall decrease of 3.8% in applications in the European Union (there were 396,737 applications for asylum in 1999).

It is often assumed that applications rise year on year in Europe and the figures above show this is not the case.

The early 1990s

In the early 1990s there was a rise in asylum applications in Europe.* This was due in the main to the Balkan wars and the resultant rise in applications from the countries of former Yugoslavia, as well as from Romania and Turkey. Applications from former Yugoslavia accounted for just under a quarter of applications during the five years 1990-1994.

*Figures for Europe are for the following countries: Austria, Belgium, Bulgaria, Czech Republic, Cyprus, Denmark, Estonia, Finland, France, Germany, Greece, Hungary, Iceland, Ireland, Italy, Latvia, Liechtenstein, Lithuania, Luxembourg, Malta, Netherlands, Norway, Poland, Portugal, Romania, Slovakia, Slovenia, Spain, Sweden, Switzerland, Turkey and the United Kingdom.

The late1990s

In the late 1990s there was again a rise in applications in Europe during the Kosovo crisis when applications from the Federal Republic of Yugoslavia increased to 98,270 in 1998

and 121,333 in 1999 as compared with 48,402 in 1997. There was also a notable increase in applications for asylum in Europe from Iraq, a trend which would continue into the 2000s.

2000-2002

The early years of the 2000s saw an increase in applications from Afghanistan, peaking in 2001 at just under 50,000 and almost doubling in a year from 29,928 in 2000. Meanwhile applications from Iraq dramatically increased in the early 2000s, culminating in 50,058 in 2002.

Where do asylum seekers in Europe come from?

The four main countries of origin of asylum seekers in Europe in 2002 were Iraq with 50,058 applications, Federal Republic of Yugoslavia with 32,656 applications, Turkey with 28,455 applications and Afghanistan with 25,470 applications.

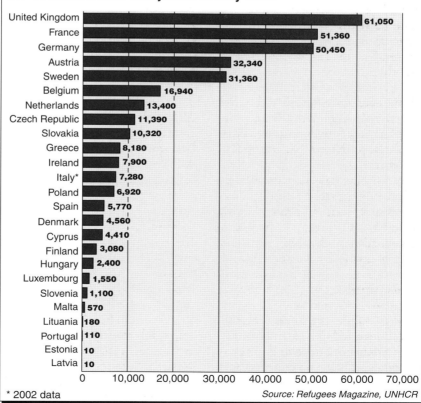

Asylum requests

Asylum requests in European Union countries in 2003, including the 10 latest states that joined in May 2004

United Kingdom	61,050
France	51,360
Germany	50,450
Austria	32,340
Sweden	31,360
Belgium	16,940
Netherlands	13,400
Czech Republic	11,390
Slovakia	10,320
Greece	8,180
Ireland	7,900
Italy*	7,280
Poland	6,920
Spain	5,770
Denmark	4,560
Cyprus	4,410
Finland	3,080
Hungary	2,400
Luxembourg	1,550
Slovenia	1,100
Malta	570
Lituania	180
Portugal	110
Estonia	10
Latvia	10

* 2002 data

Source: Refugees Magazine, UNHCR

Iraq, Human Rights Watch World Report 2003

'The Iraqi government continued to commit widespread and gross human rights violations, including the extensive use of the death penalty and the extrajudicial execution of prisoners, the forced expulsion of ethnic minorities from government-controlled areas in the oil-rich region of Kirkuk and elsewhere, the arbitrary arrest of suspected political opponents and members of their families, and the torture and ill-treatment of detainees.'

Federal Republic of Yugoslavia, Amnesty International Report 2003

'The authorities largely failed to address impunity for war crimes in Bosnia-Herzegovina, Croatia and Kosovo. Detainees were frequently ill-treated and sometimes tortured in police custody, allegedly resulting in at least one death in custody. Roma, especially internally displaced people (IDPs) from Kosovo, continued to face severe discrimination. An estimated 230,000 Serbian and Romani IDPs from Kosovo remained in the Federal Republic of Yugoslavia (FRY), along with 390,000 refugees from Bosnia-Herzegovina and Croatia.'

Afghanistan, Amnesty International Report 2003

'Grave human rights abuses and armed conflict continued. Hundreds of people were arbitrarily detained and held in poor prison conditions. Impunity remained entrenched and perpetrators of human rights violations largely went unpunished. Violence continued with factional fighting between regional commanders and armed militias. Mass graves were discovered. Despite the lifting of restrictions on their freedom of movement, women feared for their security and were subjected to acts of violence, rape, public harassment and intimidation.'

Turkey – an excerpt from the US Department of State Human Rights Report 2002 on Turkey

'The Government generally respected the human rights of its citizens; although there were improvements

---

The four main countries of origin of asylum seekers in Europe in 2002 were Iraq, Federal Republic of Yugoslavia, Turkey and Afghanistan

---

in a number of areas, several serious problems remained. Security forces continued to commit unlawful killings, including deaths due to excessive use of force and torture. Torture, beatings, and other abuses by security forces remained widespread, although the number of reported cases declined. There were reports that police and Jandarma often employed torture and abused detainees during incommunicado detention and interrogation. The lack of universal and immediate access to an attorney, long detention periods for those held for political crimes, and a culture of impunity were major factors in the commission of torture by police and security forces. The rarity of convictions and the light sentences imposed on police and other security officials for killings and torture continued to foster a climate of impunity. Prison conditions remained poor, despite some improvements. According to the Human Rights Association (HRA), 26 persons died during the year as a result of the continuing hunger strikes to protest new small-cell prisons. Police and Jandarma continued to use arbitrary arrest and detention, although the number of such incidents declined slightly. Prolonged pretrial detention and lengthy trials continued to be

problems. Prosecutions brought by the Government in State Security Courts (SSCs) reflected a legal structure that protects state interests over individual rights.'

Which European countries have the highest number of asylum applications?

When the number of asylum applications are compared with the total population of the state in which the applications are made (i.e. applications per 1000 inhabitants), in 2002, out of 25 European countries, Austria was the European country with the highest ratio of applications to population with 4.6 applications per 1000, followed by Norway (3.9), Sweden (3.7), Switzerland (3.7), Ireland (3.1) and Liechtenstein (2.8). Germany had 0.9 applications per 1000 inhabitants and the UK 1.9.

A further useful indicator is a comparison between the average number of applicants per 1000 inhabitants in the European Union in the decade between 1992 and 2001. Sweden ranks the highest at an average of 2.57 applicants per 1000 inhabitants between 1992 and 2001, the Netherlands second (2.27), Belgium third (2.16) and Germany fourth (1.94). The United Kingdom comes ninth with 0.97 applicants per 1000 inhabitants (source: *Number of asylum applicants sub-mitted in 30 industrialized countries, 1992-2001*).

In 2002, according to available statistics, the United Kingdom received the most asylum applications in Europe with 110,700 applications, followed by Germany with 71,127.

For the period 1992 to 2002, Germany recorded 1,668,398 new applications for asylum, nearly half the total applications in Europe for that period.

■ The above information is an extract from *Introduction to Asylum in Europe*, a factsheet produced by European Council on Refugees and Exiles (ECRE). For further information visit their website at www.ecre.org

Refugees: young people speak out

How do the opinions of adults and youngsters differ on the subject of asylum seekers? As National Refugee Week 2003 got under way, we asked Islington-based news agency Children's Express to find out.

National Refugee Week in June 2003 focused on children and young people.

A survey conducted last year found young people in Britain were more likely than adults to have negative feelings about refugees and asylum seekers. Children's Express, the Islington-based news agency, decided to ask young people for their views.

Haifa, 17, said: 'I don't think the financial support asylum seekers get in Britain is as much as everyone makes out. I think they only get about £30 a week to survive on, which isn't much.

'Also a lot of the people who come here are highly qualified. They've been doctors or lawyers in their own country but they come here and they're forced to do jobs which involve less skill for a lot less money.'

One 17-year-old who asked not to be named said: 'My Mum's not very keen on refugees. She's got quite traditional views. She's always complaining about them because near our house there are some council flats and lots of asylum seekers move in. She thinks they don't respect their property and other residents. She doesn't mind genuine refugees, it's illegal immigrants she says she doesn't like.'

'If they print a headline saying "1000 Asylum Seekers Coming" people get worried and think "Oh they're going to take our jobs and our flats"'

Conrad, nine, said: 'Refugees and asylum seekers come to the UK because they don't have enough rights in their own country and they know there's no war here and they know it's going to be safe. But the newspapers write a lot of negative stuff about them.

'If they print a headline saying "1000 Asylum Seekers Coming" people get worried and think "Oh they're going to take our jobs and our flats".'

Tara, 14, said: 'When black and Irish people first started to come to England, there were signs up that said "No Dogs, No Blacks, No Irish." That was extreme stuff. A lot of these immigrants helped to develop this country by doing manual labour – building hospitals and driving buses. They did their bit to help society. If we give the people who are coming here now the same chance, they can be helpful as well.'

Carmen, 14, said: 'I don't know if I agree with the findings of the survey done during Refugee Week 2002 that young people are more likely to have negative opinions about asylum seekers. It does depend on where you live.

'I think the way the media portrays the issue is negative and very unfair which doesn't help matters. Young people are more likely to believe the things they read because we've got less experience in the world.'

About the team

This story was produced by Jimmy Tam, 18, and Horia El Hadad, 17. It was published in the *Highbury and Islington Express*.

■ The above information is from the Children's Express website: www.childrens-express.org

© *Children's Express*

Asylum – myths and facts

Information from the Medical Foundation for the Care of Victims of Torture

The Medical Foundation is a human rights charity that works with survivors of torture and organised violence. Those seeking our help include, among others, former Far East prisoners of the Japanese in WWII and aid workers and journalists who have been caught up in tumultuous world events. However, the vast majority of our clients are people who have fled persecution in their countries of origin to arrive in the United Kingdom as asylum seekers. Our torture survivor clients experience the same difficulties in this country as other asylum seekers. Moreover, torture survivors may suffer especially because of past horror and present vulnerability. Some could die if returned to the country where they were tortured; others fear removal so much that they attempt to commit suicide here in the UK. There is much misinformation surrounding the issue of asylum, so here we examine some of the popular myths that adversely affect the well-being of asylum seekers, among whom are our clients.

Myth: Almost all asylum seekers are bogus

Fact: Nearly half of all asylum claimants in 2002 were granted the right to stay

According to Home Office statistics [published 22 May 2003] there were 82,715 initial asylum decisions made in 2002. Some 10 per cent were granted refugee status with a further 24 per cent being granted Exceptional Leave to Remain (ELR) – meaning more than one-third of all claimants (28,125) who received an initial decision in 2002 were accepted outright as having a legitimate claim to stay in this country. In addition, the Home Office received 49,500 appeals against decisions it had made in 2002. Adjudicators, working hard to clear a backlog of appeals, ruled on some

Caring for victims of torture

MEDICAL FOUNDATION

www.torturecare.org.uk

64,405 cases – overturning 24% of Home Office decisions in favour of those seeking asylum. When this rate of appeal success is applied to the 49,500 figure of 2002 appeals, we find that a further 11,880 asylum seekers were granted refugee status (14% of all initial Home Office asylum decisions in 2002). Add this group to the initial 34% given refugee status or ELR and it becomes clear that 48% or nearly half of all asylum claimants in 2002 were recognised as having the legitimate right to remain in this country.

Myth: Britain is a soft touch, taking more than its fair share of refugees

Fact: Less than 2% of the world's refugees are taken in by Britain – the world's fifth richest nation

An opinion poll commissioned to mark the start of Refugee Week 2002 undertaken by respected pollsters MORI found that on average people believed Britain was home to nearly a quarter of the world's refugees and asylum seekers, when the true figure is under two per cent (1.98% based on UNHCR estimates). In 2002 the

UK did receive more asylum applications than any other West European country in terms of absolute numbers. However, in terms of asylum applications per head of population, which is a fairer indicator of the capacity of countries to host asylum seekers, the UK ranked only 8th in Western Europe in 2002, receiving just under two claims (1.9) per thousand people. Austria in fact took the greatest number of asylum seekers per capita (4.6 claims per thousand), followed by Norway (3.9), Sweden (3.7), Switzerland (3.7), Ireland (3.1), Liechtenstein (2.8) and Luxembourg (2.4) [source: UNHCR Population Data Unit, March 2003]. Compared to the size of the national population, the main refugee hosting countries anywhere in the world during 2001 – the latest year for which UNHCR statistics are available – were Armenia, followed by Congo, Yugoslavia, Djibouti and then Zambia.

Myth: Only tougher measures like stricter border controls will deter asylum seekers

Fact: Refugees are forced to flee their homelands because of conflict and persecution. Governments should direct their attention to these root causes of displacement

Home Office research (Study 259,

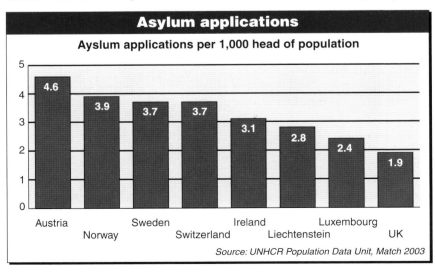

Asylum applications

Ayslum applications per 1,000 head of population

Austria 4.6, Norway 3.9, Sweden 3.7, Switzerland 3.7, Ireland 3.1, Liechtenstein 2.8, Luxembourg 2.4, UK 1.9

Source: UNHCR Population Data Unit, Match 2003

June 2003) by Professor Roger Zetter, which looks at the impact of asylum policy changes in Europe over the 1990s, finds only a 'tenuous' relationship between tougher policies and the impact on asylum numbers. It goes on to suggest that new policy measures have produced un-anticipated outcomes, including encouraging trafficking and making what had been a relatively visible and quantifiable flow of asylum seekers into a 'covert movement of irregular migrants that is even more difficult for states to count and control'. The Home Office's report argues that 'insufficient weight' has been given to other contextual factors, including the changing nature of humanitarian crises and the historical ties between countries – factors that had in fact made the flow of asylum seekers, to a large extent 'policy resistant'. This view is shared by the Institute of Public Policy Research (IPPR). In their 2003 report entitled *States of Conflict*, they conclude that 'push factors' – including repression and/or discrimination of minorities; ethnic conflict and human rights abuses; and war – are common factors among the main countries of origin of refugees arriving in the United Kingdom. In its conclusion the authors note: 'The most important need we identified is for longer-term policies designed to prevent conflict and bring about social, economic and political development.'

Myth: Arriving in Britain means asylum seekers start an easy life on welfare benefits

Fact: Asylum seekers, many of whom have suffered past trauma, may experience racism and discrimination here in exile
Research conducted by the Migration Unit of the University of Wales for the Home Office (Study 243, July 2002) found little evidence that asylum seekers 'have a detailed knowledge of UK immigration or asylum procedures; entitlements to benefits in the UK; or the availability of work in the UK'. Asylum legislation in this country means asylum seekers are not permitted to work, despite the same study finding

evidence that asylum seekers would prefer to support themselves rather than rely on the State: 'In the longer term there was near universal belief [among the asylum seekers questioned] that they would be allowed to find work in the UK. Expectations of state support were in many cases quite low, and respondents anticipated that they would have to find work to support themselves and meet living costs.' Moreover, asylum seekers who flee to Britain to find safety are often demonised, discriminated against and forced to live in fear, according to a June 2003 report by the Churches Together in Britain and Ireland (CTBI) entitled *Asylum Voices*. It draws on the personal experiences of refugees from 37 countries and tells of the 'shameful' way in which they are treated once in Britain. A report published by the Association of Chief Police Officers (ACPO) found that 'racist expressions towards asylum seekers appear to have become common currency and "acceptable" in a way which would never be tolerated towards any other minority group' (source: *Asylum Seekers Policing Guide*). ACPO concluded that 'paradoxically, it is not unusual for those seeking asylum in this country, as a safe haven, to experience racial discrimination and harassment'.

Myth: Asylum seekers get more than their share of welfare benefits and priority on hospital waiting lists

Fact: Asylum seekers receive lower amounts of benefits than UK citizens
Asylum seekers are not allowed to claim mainstream welfare benefits and fall under the control of the

National Asylum Support Service (NASS). A single adult refugee claimant on NASS support receives just £37.77 a week – some 30% below the poverty line. This compares with a single pensioner's guaranteed minimum income of £98.15 a week or an unemployed adult (over 25) who receives the jobseeker allowance of £54.65 [correct as at 1 August 2003]. The United Kingdom gives asylum seekers less financial support than many other European countries including Belgium, Ireland and Denmark. Nor do asylum seekers get preferential health treatment. According to the Department of Health, it is expected that an asylum seeker will be treated like any other UK resident as soon as they have submitted an asylum application. 'They have the same rights to access healthcare as anyone else,' a Health Department spokesman told the BBC (7 November 2002).

Myth: Asylum seekers are swamping the NHS with diseases like HIV and TB

Fact: Once settled, asylum seekers make no more demands on the NHS than the general population
Blaming asylum seekers for the larger problems of the NHS may be easy, but it is neither accurate nor fair. Derek Bodell, Chief Executive of the National Aids Trust, and Dr Edwin Borman, chairman of the British Medical Association's International Committee, wrote, with others, in a letter to the *Sunday Telegraph* newspaper (June 2003): 'It is true that individuals from other countries living, working or seeking asylum in the UK can receive NHS treatment for medical conditions. It is not accurate to say HIV-positive individuals in general, and asylum seekers in particular, are the primary reason that hospitals are facing budgetary problems . . .' Indeed, the All-Party Parliamentary Group on Aids in its report *Migration and HIV: Improving Lives in Britain* (July 2003) declared rather: 'From the evidence there was a general consensus that NHS services are over-stretched due to prolonged under-investment.' Dr Michael Peel, the Medical Foundation's Health and

Human Rights Advisor, says: 'Asylum seekers may have high demands in the short term because they may not have had access to healthcare in the past or because of the consequences of the perilous journeys many have made to reach safety. But once they become settled, their demands are no more than the general population.'

Myth: Compulsory health screening for asylum seekers would reduce infectious disease rates

Fact: Experts believe screening to be ineffective and could drive those infected underground

A new report from the London School of Hygiene and Tropical Medicine concludes that coping with international health risks by means of tighter border controls no longer works. Kelly Lee of the School said: 'Border controls might reassure the public, but they are going to be ineffective. What no one wants is to have people walking around who might be infecting others but who are not going to get checks because they are worried about their immigration status. If they disappear off the radar screen that could be really dangerous,' (*Observer* 22 June 2003).

Professor Michael Adler, a renowned HIV physician who was the Government's adviser on sexual health, agreed, noting that if the results of health screening affected a person's immigration status it could drive some people with infectious diseases underground. The All-Party Parliamentary Group on Aids was even more unequivocal. It concluded: 'It would be in breach of international obligations and human rights to give mandatory HIV tests to asylum seekers upon entry and in addition there is no evidence to support that such a policy would be effective at protecting the public health . . . Instead the Government should encourage policies on inclusion which support testing based on informed consent with the aim of reaching individuals in need so that they can receive timely access to care and treatment' (*Migration and HIV: Improving Lives in Britain*, July 2003).

Myth: The media and politicians are leading an informed and balanced debate on the asylum issue

Facts: There is widespread concern that media coverage is unbalanced, poorly researched and hostile, and that politicians have not done enough to enlighten the public about the issue

That so many myths abound about asylum seekers and refugees indicates a poor level of informed and balanced coverage of the asylum issue by the media. The Association of Chief Police Officers (ACPO), in its introduction to guidelines for better policing in asylum communities notes: 'Our experience over the last 4 years has been that where asylum communities have been established there has been ill informed adverse media coverage which has contributed to heightened local tensions and resentment of asylum seekers.' An April 2003 report by the Refugees, Asylum-seekers and the Media (RAM) Project finds widespread concern about coverage of refugee and asylum issues in the

> **There is widespread concern that media coverage is unbalanced, poorly researched and hostile, and that politicians have not done enough to enlighten the public about the issue**

UK. Respondents, who included refugees and asylum seekers themselves, those working on their behalf in refugee agencies, and many members of the media who attended a series of RAM events held between January and April 2003, were particularly concerned about the effect of coverage on the lives of refugees and asylum seekers and on community relations in the areas in which they live. Their report, *The Challenge of Reporting Refugees and Asylum Seekers*, summed it up as follows: 'While each of these groups of participants have their own particular interests and concerns, all perceived the coverage as predominantly unbalanced, poorly researched and hostile.' The European Commission against Racism and Intolerance found that our leaders were not doing enough: 'Regrettably, many politicians have contributed to or at least not adequately prevented, public debate taking on an increasingly intolerant line with at times racist and xenophobic overtones. Public statements have tended to depict asylum seekers and 'economic migrants', explicitly or by reference, as a threat to security, economic stability and social peace . . . ECRI urges the British authorities to take these concerns into account.' [source: ECRI Second Report on the United Kingdom, 16 June 2000]

■ The above information is from the Medical Foundation for the Care of Victims of Torture's website: www.torturecare.org.uk and reproduced with kind permission.
© Medical Foundation for the Care of Victims of Torture

New campaign argues case for migration

By Hugh Muir

MPs, trade unionists, business organisations and political activists were today (28 June 2004) launching a new group to defend Britain's migrants and make the case for more legal migration.

The Migration Alliance is being created amid fears that the debate about migration has been hijacked by rightwingers and anti-migrant groups.

There is particular concern about the activities of the rightwing thinktank Migration Watch, which has been accused of releasing inflammatory estimates about the levels and the effects of migration. The group's figures and conclusions are eagerly seized upon by rightwing newspapers and opponents of increased migration.

The Alliance includes the TUC, Unison, the GMB and the Communication Workers' Union. Also involved are the CBI, the Joint Council for the Welfare of Immigrants, the Immigration Advisory Service and the NHS Confederation. The launch focuses on the positive effect of migration on the health service.

Barbara Roche, the former Home Office minister, will chair the first meeting and act as the group's parliamentary coordinator. She said: 'We are in a new century of legal migration. Legal migration is a good thing economically, socially and culturally.

'Because there is insufficient debate about migration, we have a polarised debate between left and right and that means you get organisations like Migration Watch, which masquerades as an independent organisation but has an anti-immigration agenda. Migration Watch has been almost allowed to occupy this ground.'

Ms Roche said the government should consider allowing a completely independent entity – organised on the lines of the Electoral Commission – to produce figures which might gain more general acceptance.

Migration Watch sprang to prominence in 2002 when the group's assertion that two million immigrants would crowd into Britain in the next decade was widely reported.

The main basis for its estimate was the official *International Passenger Survey*, which asks those arriving at British ports whether they intend to stay for 12 months or more. Once those leaving are subtracted, that gives a net inward figure of about 180,000.

But the group's argument was attacked as flawed by the Home Office. It said the number being relied upon included British citizens returning to the country from abroad as well as foreign migrants.

More recently, the group challenged government forecasts which said migrants would add 4.3 million to the population by 2026, saying the figure would be 1.7 million higher. The headline in the *Daily Express* read 'Shock as 6 million settle in the UK.'

Migration Watch UK is fronted by Sir Andrew Green, the former British ambassador to Saudi Arabia and Syria. Its other leading figure is academic Dr David Coleman, who has been a frequent critic of the Labour government's immigration policies and an opponent of multiculturalism.

Sara Buchanan of the pressure group Article 19 has conducted research into the reporting of migrant issues. 'There was a marked dependence on Migration Watch as a source of information about migration and asylum figures,' she said.

'This is not in itself an issue, but is problematic when Migration Watch's "alternative" statistics are presented as headlined statements of fact with no contextual information about Migration Watch as an organisation.'

Campaigners in favour of migration go into battle armed with statistics of their own. According to the Treasury, economic growth rates would be almost 0.5% lower for the next two years if net migration ceased.

Trends in net migration to the UK over the past two or three years have been in line with those of our European neighbours like Germany, Sweden and the Netherlands and significantly less than for Spain, Ireland, Australia or the US.

The Home Office says legal migrants comprise 8% of the UK's population but generate 10% of our gross domestic product. They contribute £2.5bn more in taxes than they consume in services and have little or no adverse affect on the wages or employment levels of the existing population.

Calls to Migration Watch were not returned, but the organisation outlines its approach on its website. It says: 'Migration Watch is not "anti-immigration" but we do believe that the present levels of immigration, the highest in our history, are making Britain overcrowded and are changing the nature of our society.'

'We believe that the facts should be known, understood and debated. Failure by the centre ground to address them will leave the field wide open to extremist groups.'

Migration myths dispelled

Frequently asked questions

Do migrants add to economic growth?

Yes. But they also add to population. The Prime Minister recently claimed that growth would be nearly 0.5% per year less if there was no net immigration. The correct figure is 0.4% and immigrants add 0.25% to the population every year. So the benefit is only 0.15% per head per year – a trivial amount compared to the extra congestion involved.

Do migrants account for 15% of economic growth?

Trend growth is 2.75% per year. 0.4 is 15% of 2.75 so this is the same claim – it takes no account of the extra population.

What is wrong with a 'managed migration policy'?

Nothing. But, in reality, it is not managed. Nearly nine out of ten asylum seekers remain in Britain, even if they are refused. And 1.5 million visas are issued every year yet there are no checks on departure. David Blunkett has admitted publicly that 'he hasn't a clue' who is in Britain . The Government must put in place the necessary tools to be able to manage migration – notably, embarkation checks and ID cards. Until then, 'managed migration' will remain merely a slogan.

Do we need immigration to boost our economy?

Major studies in Canada and the United States have concluded that the benefit of immigration to the economy as a whole is positive but very small. The impact on Gross Domestic Product (GDP) per head is a small fraction of 1%. In Britain, congestion costs probably wipe that out since we are 12 times as crowded as the United States. It follows that the case for large-scale immigration is a matter for decision on political and social grounds. The economic case is fairly neutral.

Can we do without skilled workers from overseas?

An exchange of skilled workers is to everybody's benefit but it is not a sufficient reason for net foreign immigration at the present level of nearly 250,000 a year. In the medium term it is essential that we train and re-train our own workforce. Immigration can never be a substitute for this.

Would London collapse without foreign workers?

No. The jobs being done by foreigners in London are being done by British people in the many parts of the country where there are few, if any, immigrants. What is happening is that Londoners are, in effect, being squeezed out of London by the arrival of 200,000 foreigners a year.

Don't we need foreigners to do the jobs that British people are unwilling to do?

No. The underlying issue is pay rates for the unskilled. At present, the difference between unskilled pay and benefits is so narrow that, for some, it is hardly worth working. That partly explains why we have 1.5 million unemployed and a further 2.2 million whom the Government wishes to move from welfare to work. The Government points out that there are about 1/2 million vacancies but they do not say that there are seven times that number of British people who would like to work.

Who will pick strawberries?

There is a need for seasonal labour in the agricultural sector. There is no reason why students and others should not come to Britain temporarily for this purpose. The problem with present arrangements is that there is no check on their departure.

© MigrationWatch UK

We are frequently asked about statements on asylum and immigration, many of them false or misleading, which are constantly repeated by the immigration lobby. Here is a selection.

The Myth
'Britain (or usually Europe) has a declining population and work force.'

The Facts
The British population is officially projected to increase by 5.6 million by 2031 (85% of this is due to immigration). The work force will also increase, partly because women will be working longer, With a fertility rate of 1.64, Britain is in a completely different situation from Italy and Spain whose fertility rate is about 1.2. It is therefore misleading to treat Europe as a single entity for this purpose.

The Myth
'Britain needs migrant workers to help pay for our pensions.'

The Facts
False. Immigrants themselves grow older. To maintain the present population of working age to pensioners would require over 1 million immigrants a year up to 2050. That would double the population to 120 million and leave us with the same problem.

The Myth
'Migrants contribute a net £2.5 billion to the exchequer'.

The Facts
False. The relevant Home Office paper was heavily qualified, describing the results as conditioned on the period in which they are calculated and the country's position in the business cycle. In fact the year chosen was one in which the public sector accounts were in surplus so everyone was contributing 5% more than they took out; to correct for this deduct £1.3bn. Furthermore, Corporation Tax from shareholders resident abroad was wrongly attributed to migrants; deduct a further £0.8bn. The study also overlooked the key point that, since the early 1990s, migrants have added to our population so it ignored the cost of new facilities required and the costs of special education etc.

The Myth
'People come to Britain as asylum seekers because there are so few legal avenues available.'

The Facts
An investigation by the National Audit Office (requested by the Prime Minister) reported in May 2004 that 'There is no statistical evidence that some people who might previously have claimed asylum entered the country through other legal migration routes'.

The Myth
'In 2001 the total number of successful asylum applicants was as high as 51% (Refugee Council).'

The Facts
False. This includes those granted Exceptional Leave to Remain (ELR) – a category now abolished by the Home Secretary because it had been awarded too liberally. Over the seven years 1997-2003 just over 22% were granted asylum and a further 15% were granted ELR (now renamed Humanitarian Protection). Source: Home Office statistical bulletin 09/02 Table 1.1

The Myth
'The UK ranked twelfth in the EU on terms of asylum applications in relation to the overall population in 2001.'

The Facts
Misleading. It ignores the key point that what matters is not population but population density. England is nearly twice as crowded as Germany, four times France and twelve times the United States. We took more asylum applicants than Germany and more than twice as many as France in the year 2002. In the same year we took 29% of all the applicants who came to the EU – up from 5% in 1992. Our share of the EU's population was 15%. Even after the 40% drop in applications in 2003, we still took more asylum seekers than any other country in the Western world.

The Myth
'Britain takes only 2% of the world's refugees (Refugee Council).'

The Facts
False. The Refugee Council included the refugees in Asia and Africa and also confused a stock with a flow. The correct comparison is the number of asylum seekers coming to Britain compared to the number coming to Europe in a particular year. UNHCR figures for 2002 show that approximately 23% of asylum seekers arriving in Europe (and 29% of those coming to the EU) came to Britain.

The Myth
'Those who oppose large-scale immigration seek to establish "fortress Britain".'

The Facts
Absurd. In 2002 there were 89 million international arrivals in Britain. Of these 62 million were British nationals returning home. 14 million were nationals of the European Economic Area and 12.6 million were from outside Europe. Not exactly a fortress. The issue is not how many come to Britain but how many come to settle here, often illegally.

■ The above information is from MigrationWatch UK's website: www.MigrationWatchUK.org

© MigrationWatch UK

What's it really like to be a refugee?

Why do people become refugees? What's it like to be one? And what are the facts behind some of the myths about refugees and asylum-seekers in the UK?

The facts . . .

Compare these facts with the headlines.

- If you consider global refugee and asylum-seeking populations in relation to the host country's size, population and wealth, the UK ranks 32nd in the world.
- Taking the greatest burden are Iran, Burundi and Guinea.
- Asylum-seekers are entitled to only 76 per cent of the income support available to UK citizens.
- Asylum-seekers are not allowed to work while their applications are being processed. This means they have to rely on benefits even if they have skills and qualifications and want to work.
- The UK hosts less than 2 per cent of the world's refugees and asylum seekers.
- In 2001, 31 per cent of all asylum applications received a positive decision. The Refugee Council estimates that 51 per cent of asylum-seekers were successful following appeal and other procedures. In 2001, the majority of asylum-seekers came from Iran, Iraq, Afghanistan, Sri Lanka,

 Save the Children

Somalia, former Yugoslavia and Turkey. Serious human rights abuses occur in all these countries, including torture.

Beaten by the system

'I was 14 when I came to the UK. In Africa, my father belonged to an anti-Government party. Secret police entered our home at night and beat my father in front of me. They took him away and I was taken in a separate car to prison. The police questioned and threatened me. They beat me badly and took me to hospital. I managed to escape and went to my uncle's house. He helped me to leave the country. I still don't know what happened to my father.'

George, refugee from the Democratic Republic of Congo

Always a stranger

'People always ask me where I come from, why I came here, how I support myself. They do it because they see all this stuff on television about refugees and the Sangatte camp in France. Those centres aren't a good idea. If refugees are separated from British people, they won't learn anything. But if they live in the same area and study in the same schools, people will learn that refugees aren't bad. People can also learn about other countries and even some words in another language. Even if I live here for 40 years, I'm not sure I'll get used to it. I'll always feel a stranger.'

Qadir, 17, a refugee from Afghanistan

Work it out

'You get newspapers telling you about "all these refugees" and asking "how dare they?", but they only come here because they've got such terrible conditions in their own countries. If people were educated about what was happening over there then people wouldn't mind so much if they came, and we could actually sort out their own countries so they wouldn't have to go in the first place.'

Dave, 19, from the UK

- The above information is from Save the Children's website: www.savethechildren.org.uk

© Save the Children

Leaves of life

Britain through my eyes

By Anahita Alikhani

We see from the map of Britain that it is an island separate from the rest of Europe, made up of four countries. It's about one-fifth the size of Iran, with a similar population. The island is naturally green, sometimes an intense emerald green when the sun casts an occasional pitying glance.

Contrary to what Iranians believe, the British are mostly straightforward, loveable, warm and kindly towards others. They are, or at least seem to be, patient and polite. They like walking and wait patiently in traffic; they give way, they do not quarrel in the street or race cars or cut in front of other drivers or get in a state when they lose their way in town. There is no hurry. I have yet to see anyone hurrying in a bank or shop or hospital. They always seem to have time to queue patiently till it's their turn.

In Iran you see few elderly people out and about, but here old men and women are everywhere, well groomed, enjoying themselves. In Iran they must be content to stay in with their families. Here the old women especially enjoy chatting to strangers. First thing in the morning, rollers in their hair, they put their heads out of their front doors, like so many geese. 'Where do you come from?' 'Why did you leave your country?' 'Why did you come here?' And so on.

The design of the houses suits this curiosity well: the sitting-room windows look out over the street, so the old women can keep an eye on everyone, till they think they've got to know someone, then they start a conversation, to make sure that person's real and not imagined.

Young people are very keen on drinking and dancing. Many are highly educated, but uninterested in politics or history. They take their freedom for granted; liberty means nothing to them; only we who have spent years in prison know how valuable it is. Some young people appear in the street looking very strange. If you look at them they tell you off or swear at you. If they don't want attention, why do they make themselves look so odd, even frightening? This is what freedom means to them. They can't believe that in my country, long hair or short sleeves will get you a night in a police cell, a haircut and most likely lots of bruises – or that in my country, it's a crime to listen to lively music.

> *The government here respects the people and their rights. In my country nobody has any rights, but here even asylum seekers do*

When I first saw laughing groups of young people in the streets, drinking themselves silly, wearing skimpy clothes, I was surprised. Life without freedom is black and painful, but too much freedom causes problems for the young.

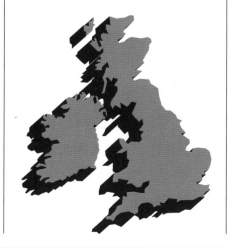

No night goes by without the television news reporting some murder or abduction. The difference in Iran is that there, the many people who are killed are mostly reporters, writers or thinkers, murdered by the cruel regime.

The main pastime here is the pub, a dark place with music from a jukebox, a billiard table, and above all, beer. No sign here of the coffee houses with their storytellers and Persian food, open till dawn. After 5 o'clock the city dies down: even London lacks the busy street life of Tehran's bright nights.

People here are given homes and unemployment benefits. In Iran they're thinking of doing this. Even the animals here are luckier than animals in my country. There are few stray animals; nobody throws stones at the pigeons or at cats and dogs. The only homeless animals here are slugs – snails without houses. I feel sorry for them because nobody takes any notice of them or asks why they've lost their homes. I have never seen so many slugs in my life. They always appear after rain.

Perhaps Mr X, who would very much like to be an Assembly Member and is unhappy because asylum seekers are lodged in furnished homes, should be thinking more about these poor snails without houses – after all they get no support from the UN. But perhaps he doesn't know what the UN is!

The government here respects the people and their rights. In my country nobody has any rights, but here even asylum seekers do. I personally am very grateful to the government and the people here. In Iran they knock you down and force you to stay at home for most of your life. The privileges here are the gift of a free society, where it isn't criminal to be critical.

■ Anahita Alikhani is from Iran. She studied Art to MA level at the University of Tehran, and worked as a tutor there. In 1998 she began working as a journalist with German, Austrian and Turkish television teams. Detained and tortured after reporting on student protest demonstrations, she fled her country in 2001.

Recently granted leave to remain, Anahita won a place on a multimedia journalism course with the BBC. She has done work on a film about asylum seekers which aimed to provide information about asylum-related issues in Swansea, where she lives. Anahita volunteers for the Welsh Refugee Council and the Swansea Bay Asylum Seekers'

Support Group (SBASSG). She hopes to be able to continue to work in the interactive media industry in this country and to make more films.

Anahita's story was first published in *Between a Mountain and a Sea: Refugee Writing in Wales*, published by Hafan Books last year. The full version of Anahita's text is available on SBASSG's website at www.hafan.org, together with the other stories published in the book. To order a copy, please email hafanbooks@yahoo.co.uk We are very grateful to Anahita and Hafan Books for the kind permission to reproduce this story.

A fair exchange

Mark Oliver reports on a scheme that is helping refugees to Britain and their hosts understand each other better

Two years ago the volunteering charity TimeBank set up the mentoring scheme Time Together, which gives volunteers a chance to make refugees feel more at home in the UK.

So far the project, which is supported by the Prince's Trust, has helped match some 300 refugees with volunteer mentors. There are schemes in London, Birmingham and Glasgow.

Below, volunteer mentor David Freer and Mussie Mengistu, his refugee 'mentee', describe their experiences of the scheme.

Both live in London. They started meeting in February last year and get together every few weeks for a drink.

Mussie Mengistu, 44, is originally from Ethiopia and arrived in the UK two years ago with his family. He was a lecturer in electrical engineering at Addis Ababa university and has been working as an electrician in London while trying to get a lecturing job.

He is married to Aikaterini, from Greece, and they have two children, aged seven and five. They live on Brixton Hill, in south London.

In my job as an electrician I work alone for most of the time or meet other refugees, so it has been hard to integrate into life in England.

Mentoring is a very good idea and I was very lucky to get David as my mentor. He's a very nice man and has really helped me.

I came here with my family from Ethiopia around two years ago and have had the same problems as any refugee: I want to adapt and integrate, but it is difficult.

Everybody has a country and everybody loves his country, but some things force you to leave

---

Throughout my education I learned English, but not spoken English, and David has helped me with that: he helped me with slang words, adult words, teaching me how young men speak – things you don't learn while studying pure English.

I did not know about society in England, and he has helped me understand it better. David himself came from Scotland six or seven years ago to London so he knows what it is like arriving here. He is a very willing person socially – even my family, they know him very well, and we exchanged gifts at Christmas.

David will call me and ask what type of problem I might have. Sometimes he helps me, he says what to do.

I had problems in Ethiopia: I used to be a member of one of the opposition parties, and when the militaristic government came into power I was put in prison and tortured. Everybody has a country and everybody loves his country, but some things force you to leave.

I was a lecturer in electrical engineering at Addis Ababa university. I was well qualified. I did my higher education in Paris and lived in France for five years. When I was there I was at college so there was no problem integrating, and it has been harder here in the UK.

Here, like many refugees, I have struggled to get as good a job as I had in my own country. But I'm trying to find a way back to my profession. I have been shortlisted for four jobs lecturing at colleges.

David has given me good information about how to write and how to apply. Sometimes he helps me when I have an application.

At the moment I'm waiting to hear for the final decision about whether I have a job lecturing at West Kent College. It would be to teach electrical engineering to students aged around 16.

My wife, Aikaterini, is from Greece, and as she is a European citizen I have had fewer problems about staying here. It is a long process but I am hoping to apply for citizenship. She has been working as a chambermaid.

I have big hopes for my children. I want them to be educated. My oldest child, you can already see, she is very intelligent. At computers she can just do anything. The language is no problem for them, which will give them a big advantage. We live in Brixton Hill but I would like to move to Kent: it would be better for the children, less populated.

I want to improve myself. Next year I plan to take some graduate courses in building and construction management.

David has told me things about Britain, and I think he has learned about my culture. We will talk about Ethiopian history and how people are living there. Here in London there are some Ethiopian restaurants we have been to.

It is good that I can share my experience and my culture, and I think he likes it very much. Maybe in the future we will even have the chance to visit Ethiopia together.

David is probably moving back to Glasgow, and we might move to Kent, so we will not see each other so often. But of course we will still keep in touch. I will go to visit him and he will visit us. Of course I'm going to miss him a lot. He is one of the important persons in my life in England.

In the future I'm ready to give my time to help other people. I've learned a lot of things from the mentoring. Maybe I will be able to help others like David has helped me.

David Freer, 28, has worked in London for several years as a graphic designer. He worked for Saatchi & Saatchi before setting up a design firm called Philosophy, which specialises in print-based design.

I got involved with mentoring to try and give something back and because I was not happy with the picture of refugees that has been painted in the tabloid press.

Mussie is a really interesting guy. We meet up every few weeks for a drink and talk about everyday things. I think that since we started meeting he's got a lot more confident about his work and applications for jobs.

He would list things that he could not understand and show me. There are so many tiny little social and cultural things that British people take for granted

---

At first I was worried about not being able to give enough practical advice, but what you find is that you help in lots of little ways.

A big thing has been helping with Mussie's conversational English: Mussie had technically great English when he came over from Ethiopia but it's another thing entirely being here and grappling with a London bus driver.

He would list things that he could not understand and show me. There are so many tiny little social and cultural things that British people take for granted.

The idea of mentoring was first put in my head when I saw an advert about it in a cinema a few years ago. The thing about living in London is that you always feel you have no time, but when I eventually found out about the Time Together scheme it seemed very flexible.

At first you do a couple of workshops doing things like role-playing and so on, to get the idea of what's involved, and then they try and match you up with someone.

The idea is that you meet up once a fortnight. We usually meet in the same place, the Royal Festival Hall on the South Bank. It seemed appropriate for the first visit, with it being somewhere open and where you really feel like you're in London.

Last month we went to a gig at the African music festival, and he's taken me to Ethiopian restaurants and I've learned things about his culture. He's a fascinating guy.

I had some empathy with what it must be like for Mussie arriving in London: I came here a few years ago from Glasgow, and it can be an overwhelming place. Just to have a friend is very important

For me, I think being a mentor has helped me feel better about living in London, better about myself. It's about your personal karma. I might walk by a beggar and not give them something, as we all have to do sometimes living in London, but at least I know that I have been doing something in my life that has, I hope, helped someone.

The mentoring was supposed to run for a year, and that ended in February, but we still meet up every three weeks and the mentoring relationship has developed into a friendship. Even if we both leave London, we'll keep in touch.

Be positive about refugees

Information from the British Red Cross

What do young refugees need?

While politicians and the press debate the 'refugee question', the simple fact remains that thousands of people are arriving in the UK asking for help. Many know no one here. Most have few belongings and little money. Some are young people, alone with no supportive family.

What do young unaccompanied refugees need?

Obviously, they want to feel safe. They may have had a terrible time, both on the journey to the UK and in the events leading up to it. They may be feeling insecure and frightened. They might have bad dreams.

But that does not mean they want to be solemn or to dwell on their problems.

Projects which work with young refugees find that mainly they just want to have fun. They want to be young and human again. They want to learn. They want to take part in sports, listen to music, hang out with friends, meet others, take on new challenges or just relax.

Such unremarkable things should be a normal part of everyday life and many young refugees yearn for simple, uncomplicated fun. The hard times they may have lived through make the need for normality greater not less.

The British Red Cross has projects in the UK to assist children and young people who have arrived in the UK and need help.

One thing these projects do is make up welcome packs for young people, containing simple things like toiletries. Such small details can make a big difference to someone who has had to leave behind everything but essentials.

What else might such packs contain? Adults are not always very good at knowing what teenagers want, but other teenagers are. What

British Red Cross

would you put in a welcome pack for a young teenage refugee to the UK? What would be a useful, friendly gift? What small luxuries might make a big difference to someone feeling alone, bewildered and desperately short of money?

You might consider putting your ideas into reality – contact a young refugee project and see if they could make use of your welcome packs. They may be grateful, especially if you could also fundraise for them.

Be positive about refugees

Refugee Week is a good time to celebrate the contribution of refugees. There is so much negative talk about asylum seekers and refugees. This often obscures the richness that refugees bring to their new countries.

Think about the United States. The country was built on the efforts of refugees – from the early Puritans

who fled British persecution in the 17th century to the successive waves of European and other immigrants. Think of all the music, film, dance, art and comedy that their energy made happen. How different would life be without that enormous cultural creativity?

Look at Britain and its refugees. There is a long list of politicians, business people, artists and musicians who are refugees or descended from them. Wouldn't life be duller without Marks and Spencer or Sacha Baron Cohen?

And what about the thousands of unnamed people who have contributed much to their local communities? In the past twenty years people have come to Britain from Ethiopia, Eritrea, Cyprus, Iraq, Afghanistan, Iran, Ghana, Sri Lanka, Pakistan, Somalia, Turkey, Congo, Burundi, Sudan, Angola, Sierra Leone, Rwanda, Kenya, Algeria, Nigeria, Zimbabwe, Colombia, the former Soviet Union and eastern European countries. The Refugee Council, who compiled this list, argues that each have brought with them a wealth of skills, languages, and experience.

It is impossible to prove, but some people have estimated that up to 75 per cent of white Londoners are descended from the Huguenots who left France because of religious persecution in the 17th century. This may be worth bringing into a discussion about Britain's attitudes to refugees.

Young people could devise art works – posters or graffiti walls – which celebrate some of the contributions of refugees. Pose questions which challenge the negativity around refugees.

■ The above information is from the British Red Cross's website which can be found at www.redcross.org.uk Alternatively, see page 41 for their address details.

© *British Red Cross 2004*

Asylum decisions

New report exposes Home Office failures causing nearly 14,000 wrong asylum decisions in one year

A new report released by Amnesty International reveals Home Office asylum decisions based on inaccurate and out-of-date country information, unreasoned decisions about people's credibility and a failure to properly consider complex torture cases.

Government figures show that the Home Office gets the initial decision wrong on nearly 14,000 asylum cases in the last reported calendar year (2002), meaning around 1 in 5 cases are overturned after costly appeals. This figure rises to nearly 4 in 10 cases from Somalia, and more than 1 in 3 Sudanese and Eritrean asylum applications.

Amnesty International UK Director Kate Allen said: 'Getting an asylum decision wrong is not like a clerical error on a tax bill or parking fine. Wrongly refusing someone's claim could mean returning them to face torture or execution. These are life-or-death decisions and the Home Office is getting one in five of them wrong.

'Our study of Home Office refusal letters to asylum seekers shows a staggering lack of accurate information about the situations asylum seekers are fleeing from. This is compounded by a negative culture that means many claims simply aren't taken seriously.

'The Government should focus on improving decision-making from the start, leading to speedier results and fewer costly appeals.'

Get it right: How Home Office decision making fails refugees, February 2004, is based on analysis of over 170 Home Office asylum refusal letters received by Amnesty International in 2003. It exposes a startling lack of knowledge about the situation in countries that people are fleeing and documents unexplained assumptions about the actions of refugees and others: for example the refusal to believe that a prison guard might help a woman escape after she had been repeatedly raped.

> *'The fact that fighting was taking place in Kisangani is irrelevant. The Secretary of State can reasonably expect you to go there.'*
> Home Office refusal letter to asylum seeker from the Democratic Republic of Congo

The organisation warned that plans announced by Home Secretary David Blunkett last year would reduce rights to appeal, with a new one-tier appeals body that is beyond the scrutiny of the law courts. New guidelines will also severely limit the amount of legal aid granted to asylum applicants, making the process of lodging a claim and an appeal even more difficult.

Kate Allen added: 'The appeals system is presently the only thing keeping thousands of people each year from persecution. When initial decision-making is so frequently wrong, reducing appeal rights against these decisions could mean returning people to face torture or execution.'

Amnesty International is calling on the Government to urgently review the decision-making process to ensure that it gets more decisions right from the very start, including:

- Better training for asylum case-workers, including external training in refugee and human rights law and country information;
- An Independent Documentation Centre to provide up-to-date and objective information on asylum seekers' countries of origin;
- A mechanism for the Home Office to reconsider wrong decisions in some circumstances without recourse to costly appeals;
- Asylum applicants who allege that they have been tortured should be referred to specialist interviewers who have in-depth knowledge of specific countries and torture methods;
- A legal representative for asylum seekers to be present at their initial interview to take their own record of the interview.

Case studies

Taken from Get it right: How Home Office decision making fails refugees

'The basis of your claim is that you fear persecution in Syria because of your political beliefs. You are a member of the Hergirtin. The Secretary of State is not aware that this political party actually exists.'
Syrian Kurd, Refusal letter

The top ten applicant nationalities – Q1 2004

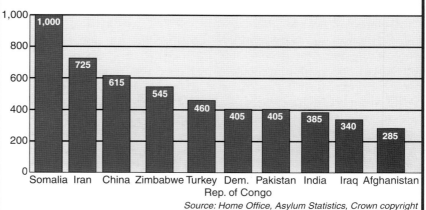

The number of applications from Somali nationals fell by a fifth (20%) from Q4 2003 but was the highest applicant nationality for the fourth consecutive quarter.

Nationality	Applications
Somalia	1,000
Iran	725
China	615
Zimbabwe	545
Turkey	460
Dem. Rep. of Congo	405
Pakistan	405
India	385
Iraq	340
Afghanistan	285

Source: Home Office, Asylum Statistics, Crown copyright

Amnesty International

According to Amnesty International's information, the 'Hergirtin' Party ('Hevgirtina Gel a Kurd li Sûriya' or 'Hevgirtina Gel') exists in Syria. The party is unauthorised by the Syrian state and therefore operates in secret. The party was founded in 1975, and was then named Partya Dêmokratî Kurd a Cep li Sûriya. It has been known as 'Hevgirtina Gel' since 1980.

In Syria, Kurdish parties are perceived as 'separatist', and involvement with such organisations at any level is a serious crime which can lead to imprisonment and torture. The consequences of return to Syria for this applicant would have been extremely serious.

'The Secretary of State considers that the authorities of Colombia are capable of offering you effective protection. With regard to the offences

committed against you, and the failure of the police to capture the perpetrators, the Secretary of State does not consider that the inability of the police to identify and apprehend such people can be construed as complicity in, or support for, such behaviour. He is aware that prosecutions are actively pursued through the courts when arrests are made.'

Colombia, Refusal letter

Amnesty International

There are approximately 20 politically related killings a day in Colombia. Amnesty International is aware that in 2003 approximately 75% of non-combat politically-related killings and forced disappearances were attributed to paramilitaries acting in conjunction with, or with the acquiescence of the Colombian Security forces. Around 8% were attributed directly to the security forces. Amnesty International continues to document the ongoing collusion between the armed forces and paramilitary forces.

■ The above information is from Amnesty International's website which can be found at www.amnesty.org.uk Alternatively see page 41 for their address details.

© Amnesty International

The economic argument

Information from Refugee Action

Perception: Asylum seekers, refugees and migrants are a drain on the UK economy.

Fact: Migrants more than pay their way in our society. Indeed, foreign-born people are a significant economic asset. Without their contribution, the average UK taxpayer would pay an extra penny in every pound in income tax.

A recent Home Office report estimated that foreign-born people – including refugees and asylum seekers – contribute around 10 per cent more to Government revenues than they receive in Government spending, equivalent to £2.5bn a year – or 1p on the basic rate of income tax.[1] Furthermore, Treasury minister Ruth Kelly has stated that the foreign-born population accounted for 10 per cent of UK GDP in 2001.[2] That is five times as much as North Sea oil.[3]

Perception: The cost of the UK asylum system has spiralled out of control and is a burden we cannot afford.

Fact: Less than one-tenth of a penny

working with refugees to build new lives

in every pound spent on public services this year will go to asylum seekers. According to Home Office Minister Beverley Hughes, the budget for supporting asylum seekers during the forthcoming financial year, 2002-2003, has been set at £434 million – just 0.1 per cent of total projected public spending for the same period.[4]

To put this figure into perspective, a recent study by the Oxford Research Group estimated that in 2001, Government subsidies to the UK arms export industry cost UK taxpayers far more – up to £990 million.[5]

Government figures for the last financial year, 2001-2002, show that the total cost of supporting asylum seekers was £1,094 million. This still represented only 0.28 per cent of total public spending.[4]

Perception: Asylum seekers come to the UK to take advantage of our generous benefits system.

Fact: Single asylum seekers in the UK have to survive on £37.77 a week – 30 per cent below the poverty line – while couples without children and single adults under 25 receive less than £30 a week each.

There are several EU countries, including Ireland, Belgium and Denmark, which offer more financial support than the UK does. A recent report for the European Commission concluded that 'push factors' such as war and repression far outweigh 'pull factors' such as economic hardship or Europe's benefits systems in determining why people leave their home countries to seek asylum in the EU.[6]

Perception: Most asylum seekers are illegal immigrants who come to the UK to live off benefits or find work on the black market.

Fact: Asylum seekers are banned from working, forcing them into the very dependence on benefits for which they are criticised. Refugees and asylum seekers represent a huge, willing and highly skilled, yet untapped workforce. A Home Office report estimates that 168,000 refugees were legally entitled to work as of August 2001.[7] In reality, most refugees in the UK are skilled and eager to work but are prevented from doing so by red tape and barriers like ignorance and prejudice.

Home Office research has found that while there is a higher proportion of qualifications and skills among asylum seekers than among the UK population as a whole, asylum seekers and refugees are consistently the most underemployed group in Britain.[7]

A major survey carried out by *Personnel Today* in November 2001 found that nine out of ten employers want to take on refugees to meet skills shortages but do not due to ignorance of the law and confusing Home Office paperwork. Almost 30 per cent of refugees surveyed had a university degree and a further quarter possessed A-level or GCSE equivalents. More than 50 per cent had more than three years' relevant work experience in their country of origin and 61 per cent had more than three months' work experience in the UK. However, 60 per cent had been unemployed in the UK for more than a year and over a quarter had been out of work for more than three years.[8]

This view is shared by the Government's own advisers. Paul Wiles, director of Home Office research, recently commented: 'The public debate over migration into the UK is often oversimplistic and ill-informed, sometimes distorted by myths about the extent to which migrants draw on our welfare state and without sufficient appreciation of the benefits they can bring.'[9]

Perception: Immigration in the UK is reaching unsustainable levels.

Fact: Home Office figures show that in 1999, the net population increase due to migration – including asylum seekers and large sub-groups such as foreign students – was 181,500.

A total of 331,800 non-British people entered the UK in 1999. The same year, a total of 268,500 people

emigrated, including 141,099 non-British people. Over the last 20 years, Britain has experienced a total net inflow of just 1.2m.[7] In 2001, the total number of people granted settlement in the UK – including successful asylum seekers – was 196,820.[10]

Sources:

1 'The migrant population in the UK: fiscal effects', RDS Occasional Paper 77, 2002.
2 *Hansard*, Written Answers, 7 May 2002, Column 33W.
3 Office of National Statistics; based on North Sea Oil output for 2001 (2.1pc).
4 *Hansard* 21 Jun 2002 : Column 623W. In addition, operating costs for the National Asylum Support Service for the last financial year, 2001-2002, were £40 million. This figure included grants totalling £18.1 million to the voluntary sector for the provision of services to asylum seekers and refugees. The NASS budget for 2002-2003 is £40.5 million. All figures rounded to nearest £million.

5 *The Subsidy Trap: British Government Financial Support for Arms Exports and the Defence Industry*, Paul Ingram, Oxford Research Group, 2001. The report conservatively estimates that each defence export job is annually subsidised by £4,200, and that over the UK defence industry as a whole, the annual subsidy paid by the taxpayer is £12,300 per job. According to Campaign Against Arms Trade, despite accounting for just 2% of UK exports, the arms trade is the most heavily subsidised sector in the UK economy apart from agriculture. UK taxpayers foot the bill for these subsidies, which amount to around £30 per taxpayer.
6 'Refugees "not chasing money"', *Observer*, Martin Bright, Sunday 26 May 2002.
7 'International migration and the UK: Recent patterns and trends', RDS Occasional Paper 75, Dec 2001.
8 *Personnel Today* and the Refugee Council, November 2001.
9 'Treasury makes 2.4 billion from legal migrants', David Leppard, *Sunday Times*, 3 March 2002
10 *Control of Immigration: Statistics United Kingdom, 2001*, Home Office Research, Development and Statistics Directorate September 2002.

■ The above information is from Refugee Action. For further information visit their website which can be found at www.refugee-action.org

© *Refugee Action*

Asylum seekers want to contribute

Refugees who arrive in Scotland have to leave behind friends and families but also in many cases a promising career. The government's policy of denying asylum seekers the right to work is a great source of frustration for people who are used to supporting themselves. Even for those who have refugee status, finding a job is often not straightforward. Mhoraig Green spoke to Dr Dilshad Kidder about his experiences as a refugee doctor.

Dr Kidder, who is Kurdish, arrived in London as an asylum seeker in 1998. Before coming to Britain he had worked as a doctor and was keen to pursue his career in the UK. He began studying immediately and passed the English language test required for him to be allowed to practise in Britain. He then moved to Glasgow where his uncle was already living.

Dr Kidder received refugee status in 2001 and although his uncle had already moved on, he decided to stay in Scotland as he enjoys the lifestyle: 'Having spent time in London, I like living in a smaller city, I enjoy being able to walk to work and Glasgow is much cleaner and cheaper than London. I feel very lucky to have settled in Glasgow because it is a good place and the people are very friendly.'

Lucky to find a job

Once in Glasgow, Dr Kidder began to study for the professional exam that would allow him to register with the General Medical Council and apply for jobs in the NHS. After he had passed this test, he got a placement at the Western Infirmary in Glasgow. He soon moved on to Monklands Hospital in Lanarkshire and eventually found a job at the Southern General Hospital in Glasgow where he has been working as a haematologist (a specialist in diseases of the blood) for almost two years now. Dr Kidder considers

himself very lucky to have found work so easily: he knows a number of refugee doctors who graduated months ago, but who are still looking for a post.

According to Dr Kidder the major difference between working as a doctor back home compared to the UK is a result of Britain's political stability: 'Here I am more focused on my work and on my patients. I do not have a constant fear of getting into trouble. I appreciate the stability here far more than the British people, because I have lived through great political instability.' Dr Kidder believes that he is a much better doctor in Britain because he has been freed from the fear of persecution.

Negative policy

Dr Kidder feels very strongly that asylum seekers and refugees should be given the right to work and should

---

The government's policy of denying asylum seekers the right to work is a great source of frustration for people who are used to supporting themselves

---

not be forced to live on state benefits. He is of course speaking from personal experience: while he was studying for his English language tests he found meeting the cost of books, photocopying and travelling to classes very difficult because he wasn't allowed to work to support himself.

Dr Kidder also resented having to live off state handouts: 'help from the government is important because it helps an asylum seeker get back on his feet. But once someone is past that stage the inability to work is devastating.' Dr Kidder was allowed to work after six months and was employed as a translator while he studied for his exams. Asylum seekers arriving in Britain today are no longer allowed to apply for the right to work and Dr Kidder believes this is a deeply negative policy: 'Asylum seekers do not want to do nothing, they want to work and make money and contribute to their new community and pay taxes. It is not only unfair to prevent a person from working to support himself, it is also humiliating.'

■ The above information is from *Finding Asylum*, the newsletter of the Scottish Refugee Council Winter 2003/4. For more information visit their website at www.scottishrefugeecouncil.org.uk

© *Scottish Refugee Council*

Serious concerns over new proposals

The new Asylum and Immigration Bill currently before parliament contains proposals that will have far-reaching implications for asylum seekers in the United Kingdom. The speed with which the bill is moving through parliament is unprecedented and it is leaving little time for serious debate or significant amendment.

Asylum is fast becoming one of the most legislated-upon areas of British law. Since 1993 the United Kingdom parliament has passed 4 major pieces of legislation relating to asylum. The current bill, presented to Parliament in November 2003, will make a grand total of five pieces of major legislation.

Such is the speed with which new regulations are introduced that asylum seekers are often unsure of how laws and policy affect them. The speed of the process also means that the concerns of the agencies who work with asylum seekers are not taken into account in the drafting of new legislation. Consultation on the present bill lasted only three weeks. Ten days later the draft bill was presented to parliament.

It is interesting to speculate on the flurry of activity there must have been in the Home Office as the civil servants sought to address all the issues raised by the various respondents in just 10 days (8 if you knock off the weekend). Such haste is a recipe for bad law, and the bill before parliament is indeed 'bad law'.

A serious attack on the rule of law in the UK

One of the most unsettling aspects of the present bill is the erosion of the right to appeal. The government justifies this by claiming that too much time is lost looking at appeals which prove groundless. However, at present one in five appeals is successful, a figure that rises to 27.4% for the main nationalities represented in Scotland. The Home Affairs

By Sally Daghlian, Chief Executive

Select Committee recently raised serious concerns about the quality of initial decisions These figures confirm that the proposed changes to the appeals system would result in genuine refugees being returned to face persecution.

A group of Scottish advocates recently wrote to the *Herald* and stated that the erosion of the right to appeal contained in the bill represented 'a serious attack on the rule of law in the UK'. In 2002 there were 15,346 successful appeals against initial decisions. Without the safeguard of the right to appeal these individuals would not have been granted leave to remain in the UK.

Without documents

The bill would make it a criminal offence to enter the UK without travel documents. While the Universal Declaration of Human Rights states that, 'Everyone has the right to seek and to enjoy in other countries asylum from persecution', the provisions in the bill would seem to undermine this basic human right

and ignore the very nature of flight from persecution. Many asylum seekers arrive with no documents or false documents for a variety of valid reasons. Irrespective of this all asylum seekers have legal status under international law. The Scottish Refugee Council believes that the 'right to seek and to enjoy asylum' should be the guiding principle of asylum law. Any attempts to erode this right should be resisted whether proposed by the UK government, the EU or any other authority.

Making it a criminal offence to enter the country without travel documents would for instance penalise those people who were unable to obtain a passport from the government that persecuted them or who had their documents taken away by traffickers. Lack of consultation is evident in the proposed legislation's failure to appreciate the reasons why asylum seekers flee and the manner by which they arrive in the United Kingdom. In order to comply with the proposals contained in the bill asylum seekers would need to have detailed information of the complex British asylum system before they arrive in the UK, when in fact most are forced to rely on the bad advice given by traffickers.

What seems to always get lost in this debate is the human impact of these measures. The Geneva Convention on Refugees was drawn up in the aftermath of World War II to ensure that future generations would have the right to escape persecution. The government is now talking of rewriting the Convention and we are unfortunately in serious danger of repeating the mistakes of the past.

■ The above information is from *Finding Asylum*, the newsletter of the Scottish Refugee Council Winter 2003/4. For more information visit their website at www.scottishrefugeecouncil.org.uk

The untapped workforce

Information from the Employability Forum

Who are refugees ?

The United Nations High Commission for Refugees (UNHCR) recently celebrated its 50th anniversary. The reasons for its continued existence and expansion were hardly causes for celebration.

Wars, civil wars and repressive regimes have forced millions of people to move from their homes in the Balkans, Afghanistan, Iraq, Iran, Sri Lanka, Sudan, Turkey, Somalia etc. The majority of those who are forced to migrate are either displaced internally or move to neighbouring countries.

There are roughly 50 million people around the world who have been uprooted. It is the poorest countries in the world that support the largest number of refugees.

A relatively small number of refugees make it to the UK. In 2001 the UK received applications from 71,000 asylum seekers. Approximately 40% of these applicants received positive decisions and were therefore given permission to work.

The Government's policy on Asylum and Immigration has been constantly changing in response to external circumstances and internal pressures. Asylum is a complex area of public policy. Despite the significant media attention it receives, little coverage is given to explain the eligibility of refugees to work in this country and to highlight the skills and experience they have to offer. It is hardly surprising that employers are often confused.

To be granted refugee status or exceptional leave to remain, according to terms defined by the United Nations, refugees have to demonstrate that they have a well-founded fear of persecution in their home country.

Until such time as their status is determined by the Home Office, they are asylum seekers. Although the Home Office is committed to giving an initial decision within 6 months, it can take longer.

In the past the Home Office generally conceded permission to work to asylum seekers who had not received an initial decision within 6 months. This concession was withdrawn in July 2002. However, those asylum seekers who had already been granted permission to work, or whose applications were in the pipeline, retained their right to work.

Research has shown that 30% of refugees have been educated to university degree level or equivalent and over 60% have been previously employed. The refugee communities in the UK include a wide range of skills and experience – doctors, nurses, teachers and engineers, as well as the semi-skilled and unskilled.

Views of employers

'In my experience refugees bring with them skills and traits that are more than welcome. They display responsibility, loyalty and, above all, a desire to learn and become economically stable – an asset for any manufacturing industry.'

Sir Gulam Noon, Chairman of Noon Products. President of the London Chamber of Commerce

'Employers now are different from the employers in the past in that they do not care about your race, background or age so long as you have the skills which are required.'

Alec Reed, Chairman and founder of Reed Executive

> ### Case profile
>
> Experienced and articulate social worker seeks position as a support worker or project worker.
>
> Previous experience includes work as a child care officer, and Head of a Children's Village in home country.
>
> UK work experience includes working as an adviser in a Citizens' Advice Bureau. Highest qualification is a BA in Applied Sociology with additional UK qualifications in health and social care.

The refugee view

'Employment serves a social function by providing refugees with a source of income; a means of making friends; an opportunity to become part of a wider network; a chance to influence local issues.'

'A job is a source of identity, self-esteem and self-realisation. It can give refugees a sense of confidence and value which will affect their whole social circumstances.'

Elahe Panahi, Trustee of the City Parochial Foundation

Overcoming barriers

Refugees face specific barriers in the UK labour market and employers can play a vital role in helping to break these down.

English language

80% of refugees speak little or no English when they arrive in the UK. English for Speakers of Other Languages (ESOL) courses are provided by Further Education colleges and by community organisations, but these courses are not always aimed at the world of work.

Employers and professional bodies can help by making it clear what standard of English is required for different levels of work. For example, the medical profession uses the IELTS exam for overseas doctors and a high standard is required and rigorously tested.

Permission to work documents

Employers must check that potential employees are allowed to take employment in the UK. Refugees do not have passports, birth certificates nor the documents which are issued to EU nationals.

Employers need to be familiar with the letters issued by the Immigration & Nationality Department (IND) of the Home Office such as:

- The Standard Acknowledgement Letter (SAL) which is stamped on the back to say that the individual is able to take employment
- The letter granting refugee status or exceptional leave to remain
- The travel document which refugees can, for a fee, obtain from the Home Office.

UK labour market

Refugees are not familiar with the workings of the UK labour market and find it difficult to understand how recruitment and selection work in practice.

Employers can make it easier for refugee applicants in the same way that they assist other 'hard to help' groups, by making it clear that they welcome applications from the refugee community and by providing work experience opportunities where this is practical.

Overseas qualifications

Refugees who arrive with qualifications from overseas find it difficult and expensive to have these translated and validated.

Employers have good links with professional bodies and can play an important role in helping refugees gain recognition for qualifications through the National Academic Recognition Centre for the UK (NARIC).

The Employability Forum
Our aims

Employability Forum was launched in February 1999 by the City Parochial Foundation to promote the employment of refugees in the UK.

Employability Forum has brought together employers, government departments and agencies, voluntary and refugee organisations to explore practical initiatives to support the integration of refugees into the UK labour market.

Employability Forum leads the work on employment and training for the National Refugee Integration Forum which was set up by the Home Office in 2001.

The main aims are to:

- influence the development of public policy on refugee integration and employment based on an assessment of the key indicators which affect refugee job seekers in the UK labour market
- develop a coherent strategy for the training and employment of refugees through an effective partnership between government, employers and the voluntary sector
- promote understanding about the key issues concerning the employment of refugees in the UK

Employability Forum is an independent charity chaired by Lord Limerick, Chairman of Pirelli UK.

- The above information is from the Employability Forum's website which can be found at www.employabilityforum.co.uk Alternatively see page 41 for their address details.

© Employability Forum

Tagging of asylum seekers

Scotland to be testing ground for tagging of asylum seekers

Key points

- Reliance Monitoring Services take on contract for tagging asylum seekers
- 70 asylum seekers in Scotland to take part in pilot
- Human rights groups claim plans would victimise law abiding immigrants

Key Quote

'Satellite tracking will also be used. Accuracy is down to inches, so we will be able to pinpoint the side of the street that someone is walking on.'

A Home Office insider

Asylum seekers in Scotland will face electronic tagging within months as part of a major security crackdown by the Home Office, *The Scotsman* has learned.

Reliance Monitoring Services, part of the same group as the security firm criticised for releasing prisoners in error, will take on the controversial contract, operating a six-month pilot scheme from September.

Home Office sources say that about 70 asylum seekers in Scotland will be involved in the compulsory trials, which will run alongside similar projects in England and Wales before being rolled out across the UK.

The idea was floated by the Home Secretary, David Blunkett, last November, but *The Scotsman* understands the trial will go ahead in the autumn.

As part of the scheme, state-of-the-art equipment, including satellite tracking, will be used to enable the security forces to pinpoint the exact location of failed asylum seekers awaiting deportation.

'The government is keen to have monitoring of all asylum seekers,' said a Home Office insider. 'They are sending a strong message . . . this is something they will have to put up with if they want to come into our country.

'Satellite tracking will also be used. Accuracy is down to inches, so

By Tanya Thompson, Home Affairs Correspondent

we will be able to pinpoint the side of the street that someone is walking on.'

The satellite equipment is the type used to monitor sex offenders on their release from prison, designed to act as a 'silent witness' in crime prevention.

Home Office sources say that about 70 asylum seekers in Scotland will be involved in the compulsory trials

It is understood that the Home Office will operate three contracts in England and Wales and one in Scotland, which will ultimately cover some 18,000 asylum seekers. It is unclear whether entire families, including children, would be tagged – a measure which would enrage some.

John Scott, the chairman of the Scottish Human Rights Centre, said the plans would victimise law-abiding immigrants who had

committed no crime. He said: 'This is completely unjustifiable unless the Home Office can prove the person will abscond. The fact that they are asylum seekers does not make them a criminal.'

Opposition politicians rounded on the Scottish Executive yesterday and accused ministers of keeping the public in the dark by leaving the decision to the Home Office.

Nicola Sturgeon, the justice spokeswoman for the SNP, said: 'The Scottish Executive are burying their heads over this, by not taking a stand against Westminster. They are dodging the issue. There are huge human rights issues here about restricting their liberty.'

A spokesman for the Scottish Conservatives added: 'The asylum system in the UK is out of control. This is another sign of the asylum crisis this government has created.'

Questions will be raised about employing Reliance Monitoring Services, a company based in East Kilbride. Although it has an impeccable record on tagging, it comes from the same stable as the private security firm Reliance Custodial Services, ridiculed for 'losing' prisoners during court escorts.

Clive Fairweather, the former chief inspector of Scotland's prisons, said Reliance had a proven track record in tagging.

He said: 'I suggested tagging asylum seekers two years ago; it seems a very good idea. Those who are genuine have nothing to fear. I can understand people having reservations ... but Reliance has been successful in the use of electronic tagging.'

Home Office staff conceded yesterday (7 July 2004) that a major public relations exercise would be needed to convince people that the action was appropriate.

'I think the chattering classes will have some problems with this, but the man in the street will accept it as a necessary measure,' said an insider.

'The issue is about legitimate applications for asylum. If these people are legitimate they have nothing to fear.'

The government has been forced to act against a backdrop of mounting criticism on the issue of asylum. Mr Blunkett has fiercely defended plans to introduce tagging, insisting it is cheaper than using detention centres and would mainly apply to failed asylum seekers. However, Labour dissidents have warned the government could face a major back-bench rebellion if it presses ahead with the plans.

The changes are expected to reduce the need for asylum centres, such as Dungavel in Lanarkshire and Yarl's Wood in Bedfordshire.

A senior Scottish police officer, who chose not to be named, said illegal immigrants were moving in and out of the country at will. 'I'm hopeful that tagging, used selectively, will bring some benefits. There is no control by the immigration service at the moment.'

As immigration is a reserved issue, the Scottish Executive will play no part in the plans and the Home Office will oversee the entire operation. But insiders say Scottish ministers are 'lukewarm' about the move.

A Home Office spokeswoman said: 'The Home Office intends to pilot electronic monitoring this autumn.'

The Executive said: 'We are aware of their general position on tagging asylum seekers. However, this is a matter for them [the Home Office] to take forward on a UK basis.'

■ Fears that Britain would be flooded by EU immigrants following enlargement were 'unfounded', Mr Blunkett said 7 July 2004 after figures showed only 240 such people had tried to claim unemployment benefits in May and June and all but six were immediately refused.

© 2004 Scotsman.com

English immigration tests will start this autumn

By Philip Johnston

English tests will be introduced for new British citizens from autumn 2004, David Blunkett, the Home Secretary, announced 8 July 2004.

Those who speak good English will be able to satisfy the requirements of the English for Speakers of Other Languages test, level three, or an equivalent qualification.

Others can attend courses combining language with citizenship, for which the better-off will be expected to pay. Applicants will be encouraged to read and write to a certain standard, and speak and understand English in a variety of formal and informal situations.

However, the Home Office said it will not be a condition of acceptance for citizenship that a particular standard is reached. Mr Blunkett conceded that not everyone could be expected to be fluent.

'But at the very least we can ask people to make an effort and to enhance their existing knowledge of English to a workable level and to know what it means to be a British citizen,' he said.

In a speech to the Institute for Public Policy Reform, in London, Mr Blunkett defended the historically high levels of immigration under Labour, which had 'enriched every aspect of British life'.

But he said the integration of new arrivals into mainstream society was crucial to break down 'barriers and false perceptions'.

'We want people from all backgrounds to feel confident about their identity and to have respect for others' identity within a positive inclusive sense of Britishness, underpinned by values we all share.'

David Davis, the shadow home secretary, said Mr Blunkett had lost control of immigration and presided over a 57 per cent increase.

Announcing a new Tory immigration strategy, he said work permits should be issued to people with 'high-value skills' needed by the economy. More than a million people under 25 were 'economically inactive', calling into question the need for large numbers of immigrant workers.

Mr Davis suggested that immigrants whose skills were most in demand should be given priority for entry. A Tory government would introduce measures to tackle the immigration 'crisis'.

They included the return of embarkation controls for non-EU travellers at all ports to check that people were not overstaying on their visas and new limits on work permits.

The Tories would also bring back the 'no switching' rule, banning people who arrived on a short-stay student or tourist visa from changing to another type of visa once here.

© Telegraph Group Limited, London 2004

Asylum seekers win back their rights

Asylum seekers win back their rights to basic food and shelter

The Refugee Council welcomes the Home Office's decision to reinstate basic levels of support to asylum seekers, even if they do not make their asylum claim immediately. Following a concerted campaign from refugee and homelessness groups through the courts the Government has revised the way it is to implement Section 55, the controversial policy which denies basic food and housing to asylum seekers who did not make their claim for asylum at ports of entry, such as Heathrow or Dover.

The decision follows a ruling from the Court of Appeal in May 2004, which found that in the case of three destitute asylum seekers their human rights had been breached. The Government has changed its policy, so that it operates more humanely, following the court ruling. The Government has indicated that it still intends to challenge it in the House of Lords but the Refugee Council's Chief Executive, Maeve Sherlock, warned against this:

'We welcome the decision to change how this policy, known as Section 55, operates. The Court of Appeal ruling found the policy of denying food and shelter to asylum

REFUGEE COUNCIL

seekers was unlawful, as they would have no other means of support. Fighting that ruling through higher courts is bound to be costly and long drawn out. We urge ministers not to pursue that course, but instead follow the logic of this change of approach, which will ensure asylum seekers have the basic essentials with which to live.

'There is clear evidence that Section 55 is causing widespread misery and destitution among people who have fled persecution in their own countries and deserve protection here. It is administratively cumbersome, which wastes valuable Home Office time that could be better spent on making high quality asylum decisions.'

The Refugee Council has long campaigned against Section 55 and

in April 2004 published a report which showed that of 130 organisations working with asylum seekers surveyed, 74 per cent had seen clients forced to sleep rough, who experienced hunger and lacked basic essentials such as clothes and toiletries.

The key findings from the report, *Hungry and Homeless*, revealed:

- 85% of respondents do not have funding to cover the cost of the services they are providing to asylum seekers denied support under Section 55 (82% of the organisations that responded are small groups with less than ten paid members of staff or run completely by volunteers)
- 74% of all organisations that responded reported seeing clients refused support even though they had applied for asylum within a few days of arrival
- 74% reported seeing Section 55 clients forced to sleep rough
- 66% reported seeing clients with health problems as a result of being made destitute under Section 55; 69% reported seeing clients with mental health problems
- 74% reported that they had clients lacking essential items such as clothes and toiletries
- 74% reported seeing Section 55 clients who experienced hunger
- 53% of respondents said they or members of their community had to provide emergency shelter for asylum seekers denied support under Section 55
- 70% of these had accommodated individuals in their own homes or those of community members.

- The above information is from the Refugee Council's website: www.refugeecouncil.org.uk

© *Refugee Council*

"Everyone has the right to recognition everywhere as a person before the law."
Article 6, Universal Declaration of Human Rights

Every child must matter in new Asylum Bill

Refugee Children's Consortium

The Refugee Children's Consortium is challenging the Government to demonstrate how its new asylum proposals square with its recent commitment to ensuring that 'Every Child Matters' and to iron out its contradictory approach to refugee children.

The Consortium, which includes the major domestic children's charities and refugee agencies, is concerned that new proposals in the Government's Asylum and Immigration Bill which gets its Second Reading in the House of Commons tomorrow (17 December 2003), will place refugee children at risk.

The Consortium is calling on the Government to treat refugee children as children first and foremost and to place their rights at the heart of asylum policy.

Under domestic and international legislation, the UK Government is obliged to ensure that decisions are made in children's best interests. However, the Bill will significantly restrict asylum appeal rights, which the Consortium fears will result in bad decisions going undetected and children being returned to countries where they are at risk of persecution.

Families whose appeal rights are restricted also face destitution under

 **Save the Children**

proposals in the Bill to withdraw all support from families whose claims have failed. The only support option will be for the family to be separated and for local authorities to take responsibility for the children. In responding to recent questions from a parliamentary committee the Home Office Minister, Beverley Hughes, admitted that this would not be in children's best interests. The organisations believe that it is completely unacceptable for the Government to try to force families to leave by making it impossible for them to look after their children if they stay. Children should not be used in this way.

The Consortium believes that the Bill provides an opportunity for the Government to provide in-

> *We welcome the Government's current agenda for children and commitment to achieving common outcomes for all children*

creased protection for refugee children and specifically to respond to recent concerns raised by the Chief Inspector of Prisons about the current policy of detaining children. The organisations are calling on the Government to end the detention of children and their families.

Alison Harvey, Chair of the Consortium, said: 'This is the fifth piece of asylum legislation in 10 years and with each Bill the situation for refugee children is worsened. This trial and error approach to children's lives cannot continue. Refugee children have experienced discontinuity and exile and should be afforded the same protection as all children.

'We welcome the Government's current agenda for children and commitment to achieving common outcomes for all children. Implementation of these proposals would betray that commitment before work has even started on realising it.

'The Consortium believes that the best interests of the child should be the overriding consideration in all decisions that affect refugee children.'

■ The above information is from Save the Children's website: www.savethechildren.org.uk

© Save the Children

- In the year 2002, there were 85,865 new applications for asylum in the UK. The nationalities with the largest numbers of applicants during 2002 were from: Iraq, Zimbabwe, Afghanistan, Somalia and China. (p. 1)

- The global refugee population fell by 10%, down from 10.6 million in 2002 to 9.7 million in 2003. (p. 4)

- A refugee is someone with a well-founded fear of persecution on the basis of his or her race, religion, nationality, membership in a particular social group or political opinion, who is outside of his or her country of nationality and unable or unwilling to return. (p. 5)

- Conflict is just one of the global causes of forced migration and displacement, and many people around the world still face persecution in countries that are not at war, such as Zimbabwe, where human rights abuses are well documented. People also flee conflict countries for other human rights reasons. (p. 7)

- In 2003, more than three million people were newly displaced, the majority by civil wars and inter-communal violence in Africa. Some 700,000 people were uprooted in the east of the Democratic Republic of Congo (DRC) alone, following a flare-up of violence in the power vacuum left by the withdrawal of foreign occupation troops from neighbouring countries. (p. 9)

- The Home Office estimate for the year 2002 was that the asylum system cost £1,800 million plus £176million for legal aid. (p. 11)

- Refugees must be granted refugee status by the UK Government before they are allowed to settle and start a new life in this country. Before this occurs they are known as an asylum seeker and are required to follow certain rules and regulations. The current asylum system is complex and the process of getting refugee status lengthy and often confusing. (p. 12)

- It is not possible to enter the UK in a legal way in order to claim asylum. Asylum can only be claimed from inside the UK. Once inside the UK, an asylum application can be made at a police station, at the Home Office in Croydon or a claim can be made to an immigration officer. (p. 13)

- In 2002 381,623 people applied for asylum in the European Union – a decrease of 1.7% (6,749) in applications on 2001 when there were 388,372 applications in the EU. (p. 15)

- An opinion poll commissioned to mark the start of Refugee Week 2002 undertaken by respected pollsters MORI found that on average people believed Britain was home to nearly a quarter of the world's refugees and asylum seekers, when the true figure is under two percent. (p. 18)

- There is widespread concern that media coverage is unbalanced, poorly researched and hostile, and that politicians have not done enough to enlighten the public about the issue. (p. 20)

- Refugee week is a good time to celebrate the contribution of refugees. There is so much negative talk about asylum seekers and refugees. This often obscures the richness that refugees bring to their new countries. (p. 28)

- Single asylum seekers in the UK have to survive on £37.77 a week – 30 per cent below the poverty line – while couples without children and single adults under 25 receive less than £30 a week each. (p. 30)

- The government's policy of denying asylum seekers the right to work is a great source of frustration for people who are used to supporting themselves. (p. 32)

- Asylum is fast becoming one of the most legislated upon areas of British law. Since 1993 the United Kingdom parliament has passed 4 major pieces of legislation relating to asylum. The current bill, presented to Parliament in November 2003, will make a grand total of five pieces of major legislation. (p. 33)

- There are roughly 50 million people around the world who have been uprooted. It is the poorest countries in the world that support the largest number of refugees. (p. 34)

- Research has shown that 30% of refugees have been educated to university degree level or equivalent and over 60% have been previously employed. The refugee communities in the UK include a wide range of skills and experience – doctors, nurses, teachers and engineers, as well as the semi-skilled and unskilled. (p. 34)

- Refugees face specific barriers in the UK labour market and employers can play a vital role in helping to break these down. (p. 35)

- Fears that Britain would be flooded by EU immigrants following enlargement were 'unfounded', Mr Blunkett said yesterday after figures showed only 240 such people had tried to claim unemployment benefits in May and June and all but six were immediately refused. (p. 37)

ADDITIONAL RESOURCES

You might like to contact the following organisations for further information. Due to the increasing cost of postage, many organisations cannot respond to enquiries unless they receive a stamped, addressed envelope.

Amnesty International – British Section
99 -119 Roseberry Avenue
London, EC1R 4RE
Tel: 020 7814 6200
Fax: 020 7 833 1510
E-mail: info@amnesty.org.uk
Website: www.amnesty.org.uk

British Red Cross
9 Grosvenor Cresent
London, SW1X 7EJ
Tel: 020 7235 5454
Fax: 020 7245 6315
E-mail: information@redcross.org.uk
Website: www.redcross.org.uk

Children's Express UK Headquarters
Exmouth House
3-11 Pine Street
London, EC1R 0JH
Tel: 020 7833 2577
Fax: 020 7278 7722
E-mail:
enquires@childrensexpress.btinternet.com
Website: www.childrens-express.org

The Employability Forum
2nd Floor, Tower Building
11 York Road
London, SE1 7NX
Tel: 020 7981 0375
Fax: 020 7981 0376
E-mail:
info@employabilityforum.co.uk
Website:
www.employabilityforum.co.uk

European Council on Refugees and Exiles (ECRE)
103 Worship Street
London, EC2A 2DF
Tel: 020 7377 7556
Fax: 020 7377 7586
E-mail: ecre@ecre.org
Website: www.ecre.org

The Global IDP Project
Norwegian Refugee Council
7-9 chemin de Balexert
1209 Chatelaine
Switzerland

Tel: + 41 22 799 07 00
Fax: + 41 22 799 07 01
E-mail: idpproject@nrc.ch
Website: www.idpproject.org

Human Rights Watch
2nd Floor
2-12 Pentonville Road
London, N1 9HF
Tel: 020 7713 1995
Fax: 020 7713 1800
E-mail: hrwuk@hrw.org
Website: www.hrw.org

Immigration Advisory Service (IAS)
3rd Floor, County House
190 Great Dover Street
London, SE1 4YB
Tel: 020 7378 9191
Fax: 020 7403 5875
E-mail: iasuk@gn.apc.org
Website: www.iasuk.org

Medical Foundation for the Care of Victims of Torture
Star House
104-108 Grafton Road
London, NW5 5ET
Tel: 020 7697 7777
Fax: 020 7813 0033
Website: www.torturecare.org.uk

MigrationWatchUK
P O Box 765
Guildford
GU2 4XN
Tel: 01869 337007
Fax: 01869 337146
E-mail:
info@migrationwatchUK.org
Website:
www.migrationwatchUK.org

Refugee Action
The Old Fire Station
150 Waterloo Road
London, SW9 0PZ
Tel: 020 7654 7700
Fax: 020 7401 3699
Website: www.refugee-action.org

Refugee Council
Bondway House
3 Bondway
London, SW8 1SJ

Tel: 020 7820 3000
Fax: 020 7582 9929
E-mail: info@refugeecouncil.org.uk
Website: www.refugeecouncil.org.uk

Refugee Women's Association Ltd
The Print House
18 Ashwin Street
London, E8 3DL
Tel: 020 7923 2412
Fax: 020 7823 3929
E-mail: info@refugeewomen.org
Website: www.refugeewomen.org

Save the Children
1 St John's Lane
London, EC1M 4AR
Tel: 020 7012 6400
Fax: 020 7012 6963
E-mail: enquiries@scfuk.org.uk
Website:
www.savethechildren.org.uk

Scottish Refugee Council
5 Cadogan Square
170 Blythswood Court
Glasgow, G2 7PH
Tel: 0141 248 9799
Fax: 0141 243 2499
E-mail:
info@scottishrefugeecouncil.org.uk
Website:
www.scottishrefugeecouncil.org.uk

Student Action for Refugees (STAR)
3 Bondway
Vauxhall
London, SW8 1SJ
Tel: 020 7820 3006
Fax: 020 7582 9929
E-mail: info@star-network.org.uk
Website: www.star-network.org.uk

United Nations High Commission for Refugees (UNHCR)
21st Floor, Millbank Tower
21-24 Millbank
London, SW1P 4QP
Tel: 020 7828 9191
Fax: 020 7630 8523
E-mail: gbrlopmi@unhcr.ch
Website: www.unhcr.org.uk

INDEX

HIV testing 20
human rights abuses 6
Human Rights Watch 6

I

illegal employment 10-11, 30-1
illegal immigrants 11, 30-1
Immigration Advisory Service 13-14
Immigration Appeals Tribunal (IAT) 14
Indonesia 9
internally displaced persons 1, 6, 8-9
Iran 1, 25
Iraq 1, 8, 9, 15-16

K

Kosovo 15, 16
Kurds 29-30

L

language
    barriers to employment 27, 35, 37
    tests 37
League of Nations 3
legal aid 29
legislation 3-4, 11, 12, 33, 39

M

Maastricht Treaty 3
Medical Foundation for the Care of Victims of Torture 18-20
mentoring schemes 26-7
Migration Alliance 21
MigrationWatch UK 10-11, 21, 22-3

N

National Asylum Support Service (NASS) 14, 19
National Refuge Week 17
NHS (National Health Service) 19-20
non state persecution 4

O

Oakington Reception Centre 13

P

passports 33
pay rates 22
pensions 23
policing asylum communities 20
population density 23
population growth 31
projects to help young refugees 28
public opinion 17

Q

Qualification Directive 4
qualifications of refugees 34-5

R

racial discrimination 19, 20
readmission agreement 4
Refugee Action 30-1

Refugee Children's Consortium 39
Refugee Council 38
Refugee Week 1-2, 7-8
Reliance Monitoring Services 36
repatriation 5, 6
Resolution on Minimum Guarantees for Asylum Procedures 3-4
right to work 32, 34
Russia 8

S

safe countries designation 4
satellite tracking 36
Save the Children 24, 39
Scotland 32, 36-7
Scottish Refugee Council 32, 33
screening interviews 13
seasonal labour 22-3
Section 55 policy 38
Seville Conclusions 4
Somalia 1, 8
Standard Acknowledgement Letters (SAL) 35
STAR (Student Action for Refugees) 12
student visas 37
substantive interviews 13
Sudan 5, 7, 8, 9
Syria 29-30

T

tagging of asylum seekers 36-7
tax contributions 23, 30
torture victims 18-20
tourist visas 37
travel documents 33, 35
treaties and conventions 3-4
treatment of refugees 6
Turkey 15, 16

U

Uganda 9
United Nations High Commission for Refugees (UNHCR) 2, 3, 6, 34
Universal Declaration of Human Rights 6

V

visas, no switching rule 37

W

war and conflict 7-8
war on terror 8
welcome packs 28
welfare support 12, 13, 14, 19, 30, 38
workforce 22-3

Y

young people, views on asylum seekers 17
young refugees 28
Yugoslavia 15, 16

Z

Zimbabwe 1, 7

ACKNOWLEDGEMENTS

The publisher is grateful for permission to reproduce the following material.

While every care has been taken to trace and acknowledge copyright, the publisher tenders its apology for any accidental infringement or where copyright has proved untraceable. The publisher would be pleased to come to a suitable arrangement in any such case with the rightful owner.

Overview

Refugees, © Refugee Week, *Asylum landmarks in Europe*, © United Nations High Commissioner for Refugees (UNHCR), *Global refugee numbers fall*, © Guardian Newspapers Limited 2004, *Asylum seeker numbers*, © United Nations High Commissioner for Refugees (UNHCR), *Refugees and displaced persons*, © Human Rights Watch, *Questions about refugees and asylum seekers*, © Refugee Council, *Fleeing the fighting*, © Amnesty International, *Reasons for leaving home country*, © MORI, *Internal displacement*, © The Global IDP Project, *Internally displaced people – world map*, © The Global IDP Project, *Asylum*, © MigrationWatch UK, *Where do asylum seekers come from?*, © MigrationWatch UK, *Refugees in the UK*, © Student Action for Refugees (STAR), *The asylum process*, © Immigration Advisory Service.

Chapter One: Refugees

Introduction to asylum in Europe, © European Council on Refugees and Exiles (ECRE), *Asylum requests*, © United Nations High Commissioner for Refugees (UNHCR), *Refugees: young people speak out*, © Children's Express, *Asylum – myths and facts*, © Medical Foundation for the Care of Victims of Torture, *Asylum applications*, © United Nations High Commissioner for Refugees (UNHCR), *New campaign argues case for migration*, © Guardian Newspapers Limited 2004, *Migration myths dispelled* © MigrationWatch UK, *What's it really like to be a refugee?* © Save the Children, *Leaves of life*, © Anahita Alikhani 2003, Refugee Women's Association Ltd, *A fair exchange*, © Guardian Newspapers Limited 2004, *Be positive about refugees*, © British Red Cross 2004, *Asylum decisions*, © Amnesty International, *The top ten applicant nationalities*, © Crown copyright is reproduced with the permission of Her Majesty's Stationery Office, *The economic argument*, © Refugee Action, *Asylum seekers want to contribute*, © Scottish Refugee Council, *Serious concerns over new proposals*, © Scottish Refugee Council, *The untapped workforce*, © Employability Forum, *Tagging of asylum seekers*, © 2004 Scotsman.com, *English immigration tests will start this autumn*, © Telegraph Group Limited, London 2004, *Asylum seekers win back their rights*, © Refugee Council, *Every child must matter in new Asylum Bill*, © Save the Children.

Photographs and illustrations:

Pages 1, 17, 31, 36: Simon Kneebone; pages 3, 22, 34: Don Hatcher; pages 5, 27, 38: Angelo Madrid; pages 11, 24: Bev Aisbett; pages 12, 20, 32, 39: Pumpkin House.

Craig Donnellan
Cambridge
September, 2004